The
SOWER'S SEEDS

REVISED AND EXPANDED EDITION

120 Inspiring Stories
for Preaching, Teaching
and Public Speaking

FATHER BRIAN CAVANAUGH, T.O.R.

Paulist Press
New York/Mahwah, N.J.

Cover design by Sharyn Banks
Book design by Lynn Else

Library of Congress Cataloging-in-Publication Data

   The sower's seeds : 120 inspiring stories for preaching, teaching and public speaking / [edited by] Brian Cavanaugh.—Rev. and expanded ed.
      p. cm.
   Includes bibliographcal references and index.
   ISBN 0-8091-4247-3 (alk. paper)
   1. Homiletical illustrations. 2. Catholic preaching. I. Cavanaugh, Brian, 1947-

   BV4225.3 .S67 2004
   251'.08—dc22

                                                                    2003016457

Published by Paulist Press
997 Macarthur Boulevard
Mahwah, New Jersey 07430

www.paulistpress.com

Printed and bound in the
United States of America

Contents

DEDICATION

*This book is dedicated to Father Augustine Donegan, T.O.R.,
who showed me the importance of writing down quotes and stories,
and to the late Earl Nightingale who encouraged
and inspired me to publish them.*

ACKNOWLEDGMENT

I am grateful for the support from family, friends, students and people-in-the-pew who have listened to my stories and encouraged me to pursue getting them published.

I thank Barbara VanDenBerg, Ann Baublis, Julie Sand, Donna Menis and Kenny Resinski for their help in identifying story themes. I especially thank Donna Menis for her invaluable proofreading and editing skills.

I am indebted to Father Bede Hines, T.O.R., for being my "coach" during this adventure.

INTRODUCTION

"To Tell a Story"

The master gave his teaching in parables and stories, which his disciples listened to with pleasure—and occasional frustration, for they longed for something deeper.

The master was unmoved. To all their objections he would say, "You have yet to understand that the shortest distance between a human being and Truth is a story."[1]

M. Scott Peck in his memorable book, *The Road Less Traveled,* begins with a most candid sentence, "Life is difficult." To continue this thought, I would add that storytelling is also difficult. What makes storytelling difficult is that it can be demanding and frustrating.

It is demanding to find just the right story for a particular occasion, and frustrating in not always being sure how the story is being received by the listeners. However difficult it might seem at times, storytelling frequently enriches and enlivens the teller of the story more than the listeners.

By reflecting on the way Jesus of Nazareth, a master storyteller, told a parable or a story and envisioning the event being described, one can sense how storytelling points to a greater reality. "It is an approach to life which we have been in danger of losing, this sense of allowing the extraordinary to break in on the ordinary."[2]

Those who tell stories—preachers, teachers or public speakers—are men and women who envision and attempt to disclose the transcendence of the immanent, as well as the immanence of the

1

transcendent in the daily lives of their listeners. "If we can rediscover this vision, then we too may be able to transform what lies to hand, let the mundane become the edge of glory, and find the extraordinary in the ordinary."[3]

Among the requirements for storytelling are the "child-like" qualities of wonder, imagination and creativity that empower one to perceive a greater reality within the ordinary daily activities of life. Zig Ziglar states that the most powerful nation is one's imagination. However, as one grows older it becomes increasingly difficult to maintain these qualities of wonder, imagination and creativity.

There was a study performed to measure a person's level of creativity. The results were that persons aged forty measured 2% creativity; persons aged seventeen measured 10%; and five year olds measured a 90% level of creativity.[4] Storytellers, therefore, have to be vigilant that they do not develop cataracts of the spirit, nor arthritis of the mind.

One of the frustrations a storyteller has to confront is the uncertainty, at times, about whether he or she is getting the message across to the listeners. The transmitter (storyteller) is sending out a signal (story) but to what frequency is the receiver (listener) tuned?

What can bring solace in dealing with such feelings of frustration is the parable "The Seed Grows of Itself" found in Mark 4:26–29: "…[S]omeone would scatter seed on the ground, and would sleep and rise night and day, and the seed would sprout and grow, he does not know how."

The telling of stories is like the farmer who scatters the seeds. The stories contain within themselves a dynamic life-force capable of sprouting, growing and bearing fruit in the lives of the listeners without the storyteller knowing how it happens. It is, therefore, the primary task of a storyteller simply to keep telling stories, like the farmer who scatters the seed.

The growth and the harvest may not be seen by the storyteller, but he or she can be assured that, if the soil of the mind and spirit is fertile, the stories will sprout and they will bear abundant fruit.

To be an effective storyteller one, in a sense, has to enter into the story. Martin Buber tells the story of his grandfather who was asked to relate a story about his great teacher, the famous and holy Baal Shem Tov.

> The paralyzed grandfather replied by telling how the holy man used to jump up and down and dance when he was praying. Being swept up in the fervor of the narrative, the grandfather, himself, stood up and began to jump and dance to show how the master had done it. At that moment the grandfather was completely healed of his paralysis.[5]

Now that is an example of entering fully into the story. Telling a story might not be as dramatic an experience for everyone as it was for the grandfather; however, a storyteller needs to remember that most communication occurs via non-verbal transmissions.

Stories are meant to be told, not read. They demand consideration of one's gesture, voice inflection, posture, tempo and facial expression. As Marshall McLuhan has rightly said, "The medium is the message."

A story is created by word-pictures much like a language that is comprised of a picture-symbol alphabet. The story unfolds scenes in the mind of the hearer that take on a form as if they were on videotape. How the story is told becomes a positive or a negative influence on the quality of the word-picture that the person hears and assimilates.

Yes, it is demanding and difficult to be a storyteller. But to feel, in the process of the telling, the scintillation, even once, of a story surging through the fiber of one's self effecting a sense of "being swept up in the fervor of the narrative" is all that is needed for the man or woman—preacher, teacher or public speaker—to discover the vitality in the story that enriches and enlivens the teller as much as the listener.

The Storyteller's Creed[6]
by Robert Fulghum

I believe that imagination is stronger than knowledge,
That myth is more potent than history,
That dreams are more powerful than facts,
That hope always triumphs over experience,
That laughter is the only cure for grief,
And I believe that love is stronger than death.

NOTES

1. Anthony de Mello, S.J., *One Minute Wisdom,* New York: Doubleday, 1986, p. 23.
2. Esther de Waal, "The Extraordinary in the Ordinary," *Weavings,* May/June 1987, p. 8.
3. *Ibid.,* p. 15.
4. Glenn VanEkeren, ed., *The Speaker's Sourcebook,* Englewood Cliffs, N.J.: Prentice-Hall, 1988, p. 106.
5. Martin Buber, source unknown.
6. Robert Fulghum, *All I Really Need to Know I Learned in Kindergarten,* New York: Villard Books, 1988, p. 1.

1. Cure for Sorrow

Anonymous

There is an old Chinese tale about the woman whose only son died. In her grief, she went to the holy man and said, "What prayers, what magical incantations do you have to bring my son back to life?"

Instead of sending her away or reasoning with her, he said to her, "Fetch me a mustard seed from a home that has never known sorrow. We will use it to drive the sorrow out of your life." The woman went off at once in search of that magical mustard seed.

She came first to a splendid mansion, knocked at the door, and said, "I am looking for a home that has never known sorrow. Is this such a place? It is very important to me."

They told her, "You've certainly come to the wrong place," and began to describe all the tragic things that had recently befallen them.

The woman said to herself, "Who is better able to help these poor, unfortunate people than I, who have had misfortune of my own?" She stayed to comfort them, then went on in search of a home that had never known sorrow. But wherever she turned, in hovels and in palaces, she found one tale after another of sadness and misfortune. Ultimately, she became so involved in ministering to other people's grief that she forgot about her quest for the magical mustard seed, never realizing that it had, in fact, driven the sorrow out of her life.

2. Giving Calhoun the Ball

Anonymous

There once was this important football game. One team was much larger than the other. The larger team was dominating the game and beating the smaller team. The coach for the smaller team saw that his team was not able to contain or block the larger team. So his only hope was to call the plays that went to Calhoun, the fastest back in the area, who could easily outrun the larger players once he broke free.

So the coach talked with his quarterback about giving the ball to Calhoun and letting him run with it. On first play the coach was excited, but Calhoun did not get the ball. The second play was again signaled for Calhoun, but once again Calhoun did not get the ball. Now the game was in the final seconds with the smaller team's only hope being for Calhoun to break free and score the winning touchdown. The third play and again Calhoun did not get the ball. The coach was very upset, so he sent in the play again for the fourth and final down. The ball was snapped and the quarterback was sacked, ending the game. The coach was furious as he confronted the quarterback: "I told you four times to give the ball to Calhoun and now we've lost the game."

The quarterback stood tall and told the coach, "Four times I called the play to give the ball to Calhoun. The problem was that Calhoun did not want the ball."

3. Lost His Doxology

Fred Craddock

Once in a while there is a seminarian who gives up. Not suddenly, but rather slowly, zeal cools, faith weakens, appetite for Christian enterprise disappears, the wellspring dries up, the soul becomes parched and the eyes droop gloomy and listless. What happened? Did evil storm the seminarian's citadel and take over? No. Did much study drive him or her into doubt? No. Did attractive alternatives to ministry turn the head? No. Nothing quite so dramatic. The seminarian simply made the fatal error of assuming that spending so much time talking about God was an adequate substitute for talking with God. He lost his doxology and spiritual death followed.

"For it is from him, through him and to him are all things. To him be glory for ever. Amen."

4. The Acorn Planter

Jean Giono

In the 1930s a young traveler was exploring the French Alps. He came upon a vast stretch of barren land. It was desolate. It was forbidding. It was ugly. It was the kind of place you hurry away from. It had been devastated during World War I.

Then, suddenly, the young traveler stopped dead in his tracks. In the middle of this vast wasteland was a bent-over old man. On his back was a sack of acorns. In his hand was a four-foot length of iron pipe.

The man was using the iron pipe to punch holes in the ground. Then from the sack he would take an acorn and put it in the hole. Later, the old man told the traveler, "I've planted over 100,000 acorns. Perhaps only a tenth of them will grow." The old man's wife and son had died, and this was how he chose to spend his final years. "I want to do something useful," said Elzeard Bouffier.

Twenty-five years later the now not-as-young traveler returned to the same desolate area. What he saw amazed him. He could not believe his eyes. The land was covered with a beautiful forest two miles wide and five miles long. Birds were singing, animals were playing and wildflowers perfumed the air.

The traveler stood there recalling the desolate area that once was; a beautiful oak forest stood there now—all because someone cared.

5. Patience to Learn

Anonymous

A young man presented himself to the local expert on gems and said he wanted to become a gemologist. The expert brushed him off because he feared the youth would not have the patience to learn. The young man pleaded for a chance. Finally, the expert consented and told the youth, "Be here tomorrow."

The next morning the expert put a jade stone in the boy's hand and told him to hold it. The expert then went about his work, cutting, weighing and setting gems. The boy sat quietly and waited.

The following morning the expert again placed the jade stone in the youth's hand and told him to hold it. On the third, fourth and fifth days, the expert repeated the exercise and the instructions.

On the sixth day, the youth held the jade stone, but he could no longer stand the silence. "Master," he asked, "when am I going to learn something?"

"You'll learn, " the expert replied and went about his business.

Several more days went by and the youth's frustration mounted. One morning as the expert approached and beckoned for him to hold out his hand, he was about to blurt out that he could go on no longer. But as the master placed the stone in the youth's hand, the young man exclaimed without looking at his hand, "This is not the same jade stone!"

"You have begun to learn," said the master.

6. Mystery of God

William Jennings Bryan

Have you ever observed the power of the watermelon seed? It has the power of drawing from the earth and through itself 200,000 times its own weight! Can you tell me how it takes this material and out of it colors an outside surface beyond the imitation of art, and then forms inside itself a white rind, and within that, a red heart, thickly inlaid with black seeds, each of which in turn is capable of drawing through itself 200,000 times its own weight?

When you can explain to me the mystery of the simple watermelon, then you can ask me to explain to you the mystery of God.

7. Legend of the Thorn Bird

Colleen McCullough

There is a legend about a bird that sings just once in its life, more sweetly than any other creature on the face of the earth. From the moment it leaves the nest it searches for a thorn tree, and does not rest until it has found one. Then, singing among the savage branches, it impales itself upon the longest, sharpest spine. And, dying, it rises above its own agony to outsing the lark and the nightingale. One superlative song, existence the price. But the whole world stills to listen, and God in his heaven smiles. For the best is only bought at the cost of great pain.

Or so says the legend.

8. St. Francis and the Novice

Anonymous

Consider the case of the novice who wanted to possess a book of psalms. He desired to pray the psalms more often and meditate on them during the course of the day. But Francis was reluctant to give him permission....Francis said, "After you have a psalter, you will desire a breviary. Then you will sit in your chair, like a great prelate, and say to your brother, 'Bring me my breviary.'"

When the novice still did not get the point, Francis said, "My dear friend, in the past we had great heroes and warriors...and many famous knights. They endured great trials and faced bitter hardships....Nowadays some bards go around who try to obtain honor, not by doing what these great men have done, but by singing about them. This may also be your temptation. Once you start reading books and talking about them, you will put your confidence in knowledge and not in virtuous deeds."

9. Love for Others: A Hasidic Story

Anonymous

A wealthy Jewish merchant treats a poor old man with rudeness and disdain as they travel together on a train. When they arrive at their common destination, the merchant finds the station thronged with pious Jews waiting in ecstatic joy to greet the arrival of one of the holiest rabbis in Europe, and learns to his chagrin that the old man in his compartment is that saintly rabbi.

Embarrassed at his disgraceful behavior and distraught that he missed a golden opportunity to speak in privacy to a wise and holy man, the merchant pushes his way through the crowd to find the old man. When he reaches him, he begs the rabbi's forgiveness and requests his blessing. The old rabbi looks at him and replies, "I cannot forgive you. To receive forgiveness you must go out and beg it from every poor old person in the world."

10. Refusing to Accept Failure

Anonymous

Sir Edmund Hillary was the first man to climb Mount Everest. On May 29, 1953, he scaled the highest mountain then known to man—29,000 feet straight up. He was knighted for his efforts. He even made American Express card commercials because of it! However, until we read his book, *High Adventure*, we don't understand that Hillary had to grow into this success. You see, in 1952 he started up Mount Everest on his first attempt and he failed. A few weeks later a group in England asked him to address its members. Hillary walked on the stage to thunderous applause. The audience was recognizing an attempt at greatness, but Edmund Hillary saw himself as a failure. He moved away from the microphone and walked to the edge of the platform. He made a fist and pointed at a picture of the mountain. He said in a loud voice, "Mount Everest, you beat me the first time, but I'll beat you the next time because you've grown all you are going to grow…*but I'm still growing!*"

11. Parable of the Cave

Paula Ripple

Three wise men were encouraged to find what had been called the cave of wisdom and life. They made careful preparations for what would be a challenging and arduous journey. When they reached the place of the cave, they noted a guard at the entrance. They were not permitted to enter the cave until they had spoken with the guard. He had only one question for them, and he demanded that they answer only after talking it over with one another. He assured them that they would have a good guide to lead them through the regions of the cave. His question was a simple one, "How far into the cave of wisdom and life do you wish to go?"

The three travelers took counsel together and then returned to the guard. Their response was, "Oh, not very far. We just want to go far enough into the cave so that we can say that we have been there."

The response of the guard manifested none of his great disappointment as he summoned someone to lead the three seekers a short distance into the cave, and then watched them set out again after a very short time, set out to make the journey back to their own land.

12. On Judging Others

Anonymous

A brother committed a fault. A council was called to which Abba Moses was invited, but he refused to attend. Then the superior sent someone to say to him, "Come, for everyone is waiting for you."

So Abba Moses got up and went. He took a leaking jug, filled it with water and carried it with him. The others came out to meet him and asked, "What is this, Father?"

The old man said to them, "My sins run out behind me, and I do not see them, and today I am coming to judge the error of another." When they heard this they said no more to the brother, but forgave him instantly.

13. On Compassion

Anonymous

Three old men, one of whom had a bad reputation, came one day to Abba Achilles. The first old man asked him, "Father, make me a fishing net."

"I will not make you one," Abba replied.

Then the second said, "Of your charity make one, so that we have a souvenir of you in the monastery."

But Abba Achilles said, "I do not have time"

Then the third one, who had the bad reputation, said, "Make me a fishing net, Father."

Abba Achilles answered him at once, "For you, I will make one."

Then the two other old men asked him privately, "Why did you not want to do what we asked you, but you promised to do what he asked?"

Abba Achilles gave them this answer: "I told you I would not make one, and you were not disappointed, since you thought that I had no time. But if I had not made one for him, he would have said, 'The old man has heard about my sin, and that is why he does not want to make me anything,' and so our relationship would have broken down. But now I have cheered his soul, so that he will not be overcome with grief."

14. Pray Without Ceasing

Anonymous

Some monks, who had an overly spiritualized approach to prayer, went to see Abba Lucius. The abba asked them, "What is your manual work?"

They said, "We do not touch manual work, but as the apostle says, we pray without ceasing."

Abba asked them if they did not eat, and they replied that they did. "So," he said to them, "when you are eating, who prays for you then?" He asked if they did not sleep, and they replied that they did. And he said to them, "When you are asleep, who prays for you then?" They could not find any answer to give him.

Abba Lucius said to them, "Forgive me, but you do not act as you speak. I will show you how, while doing my manual work, I will pray without interruption. I sit down with God, soaking my reeds and plaiting my ropes, and I say, 'God have mercy on me; according to your great goodness and according to the multitude of your mercies, save me from my sins.'"

So Abba Lucius asked them if this were not prayer, and they replied that it was. Then he said to them, "So when I have spent the whole day working and praying, making thirteen pieces of money more or less, I put two pieces of money outside the door, and I pay for my food with the rest of the money. The one who takes the two pieces of money prays for me when I am eating and when I am sleeping; so by the grace of God, I fulfill the precept to pray without ceasing."

15. Telling One's Own Story

Anonymous

When the great Rabbi Israel Baal Shem Tov saw misfortune threatening the Jews, it was his custom to go into a certain part of the forest to meditate. There he would light a fire, say a prayer, and the miracle would be accomplished and the misfortune averted.

Later, when his disciple, the celebrated Magid of Mezritch, had occasion, for the same reason, to say the prayer, he would go to the same place in the forest and say: "Master of the Universe, listen! I do not know how to light the fire, but I am still able to say the prayer." And again, the miracle would be accomplished.

Still later, Rabbi Moshe-Leib of Sasov, in order to save his people once more, would go into the forest and say: "I do not know how to light the fire, I do not know the prayer, but I know the place, and this must be sufficient." Once again, a miracle.

Then it fell to Rabbi Israel of Rizhyn to overcome misfortune. Sitting in his armchair, his head in his hands, he spoke to God: "I am unable to light the fire and I do not know the prayer; I cannot even find the place in the forest. All I can do is to tell the story, and this must be sufficient." And it was sufficient.

16. The Watermelon Hunter

Anonymous

Once upon a time, there was a man who strayed from his own country into the world known as the Land of Fools. He soon saw a number of people flying in terror from a field where they had been trying to reap wheat. "There is a monster in that field," they told him. He looked, and saw that the "monster" was merely a watermelon.

He offered to kill the "monster" for them. When he had cut the melon from its stalk, he took a slice and began to eat it. The people became even more terrified of him than they had been of the melon. They drove him away with pitchforks crying, "He will kill us next, unless we get rid of him."

It so happened that shortly afterward another man also strayed into the Land of Fools. But instead of offering to help them with the "monster," he agreed with them that it must be dangerous, and by tiptoeing away from it with them he gained their confidence. He spent a long time with them in their homes until he could teach them, little by little, the basic facts that would enable them not only to lose their fear of melons, but eventually to cultivate melons themselves.

17. The Sorrow Tree

Anonymous

So it was that when the Hasidic pilgrims vied for those among them who had endured the most suffering, who was most entitled to complain, the Zaddick told them the story of the Sorrow Tree. On the Day of Judgment, each person will be allowed to hang his or her unhappiness and sufferings on a branch of the great Tree of Sorrows. After all have found a limb from which their miseries may dangle, they may all walk slowly around the tree. Each person is to search for a set of sufferings that he or she would prefer to those he or she has hung on the tree.

In the end, each one freely chooses to reclaim his or her own assortment of sorrows rather than those of another. Each person leaves the Tree of Sorrows wiser than when he or she arrived.

18. The Gnarled Old Oak Tree

Brian Cavanaugh, T.O.R.

One day the woodcutter took his grandson into the forest for his first experience in selecting and cutting oak trees, which they would later sell to the boat builders. As they walked, the woodcutter explained that the purpose of each tree is contained in its natural shape: some are straight for planks, some have the proper curves for the ribs and some are tall for masts. The woodcutter told his grandson that by paying attention to the details of each tree, and with experience recognizing these characteristics, someday he, too, might become the woodcutter of the forest.

A little way into the forest the grandson saw an old oak tree that had never been cut. The boy asked his grandfather if he could cut it down because it was useless for boat building—there were no straight limbs, the trunk was short and gnarled and the curves were going the wrong way. "We could cut it down for firewood," the grandson said; "at least then it will be of some use to us."

The woodcutter replied that for now they should be about their work cutting the proper trees for the boat builders; maybe later they could return to the old oak tree.

After a few hours of cutting the huge trees, the grandson grew tired and asked if they could stop for a rest in some cool shade. The woodcutter took his grandson over to the old oak tree, where they rested against its trunk in the cool shade beneath its twisted limbs. After they had rested a while, the woodcutter explained to his grandson the necessity of attentive awareness and recognition of everything in the forest and in the world. Some things are readily apparent, like the tall, straight trees; other things are less apparent, requiring closer attention, like recognition of the proper curves in the limbs. And some things might initially appear to have no purpose at all, like this gnarled old oak tree. The wood-cutter stated, "You must learn to pay careful attention every day so you can recognize and discover the purpose God has for everything in creation. For it is this old oak tree, which you so quickly deemed useless except for firewood, that now allows us to rest against its trunk amidst the coolness of its shade.

"Remember, grandson, not everything is as it first appears. Be patient, pay attention, recognize and discover."

19. The Three Student Devils

Anonymous

There were three student devils in hell who were about to accompany their teacher to earth for some on-the-job experience as devil interns. Their internship supervisor asked them what techniques they planned to use to get people to sin.

The first little devil said, "I think I'll use the classical approach. I'll tell people, 'There's no God, so sin up a storm and enjoy life.'"

The second little devil said, "I think I'll use a more subtle approach. I'll tell people, 'There's no hell, so sin up a storm and enjoy life.'"

The third little devil said, "I think I'll use a less intellectual approach. I'll tell people, 'There's no hurry, so sin up a storm and enjoy life.'"

To which little devil have you listened lately? What are you putting off in your life?

20. Answer to Prayer

Anonymous

Years ago an old lady down south had no money to buy food. But with complete trust in God, she got down on her knees and prayed aloud: "Dear Lord, please send me a side of bacon and a sack of corn meal."

Over and over again, the old lady repeated the same plea in a loud voice. Now, one of the town's worst characters, overhearing her supplication, decided to play a trick on her. Hurrying to the nearest store, he bought a side of bacon and a sack of corn meal. Upon his return to the cabin, he dropped the food down the chimney. It landed right in front of the hungry woman as she knelt in prayer.

Jumping to her feet, she exclaimed jubilantly: "Oh, Lord, you've answered my prayer!" Then she ran all around the neighborhood telling everyone the good news.

This was too much for the scoundrel. He ridiculed her before the whole town by telling how he had dropped the food down the chimney himself. The wise old woman quickly replied: "Well, the devil may have brought it, but it was the Lord who sent it!"

21. Story to Heal

Martin Buber

Martin Buber tells the story of his paralyzed grandfather who was asked to relate a story about his great teacher, the famous and holy Baal Shem Tov. The grandfather replied by telling how the holy man used to jump up and down and dance when he was praying. Being swept up in the fervor of the narrative, the grandfather himself stood up and began to jump and dance to show how the master had done it. At that moment the grandfather was completely healed of his paralysis.

22. The Samurai and the Tea Master

Brian Cavanaugh, T.O.R.

Long ago in ancient Japan, a tea master learned an important lesson in self-acceptance—know who you are, where you are and what you are doing. As the story goes, this tea master was a traveling companion of one of the greatest samurai on a journey to a distant city. This samurai was greatly honored not only for his courage and skill, but also for his wisdom and understanding. His reputation was held in high esteem, even as far as the distant city.

The tea master was in awe of this samurai, seeing the respect he received from all the people along the journey. Therefore, when they reached their destination, while the samurai was napping, the tea master slipped into the samurai's armor and went about the city to feel what it would be like to be a great samurai having the respect and esteem of the people. The tea master enjoyed his charade. The people greatly honored him, and he felt that it was possible for him really to be a samurai.

At this time, however, another samurai was living in the region. He had a reputation for being a bully and for being cruel and dangerous. He heard of the wise samurai's arrival and set out to find him. The cruel samurai soon found the other samurai, not realizing that it was only the tea master wearing the armor of the true samurai, and challenged him to a contest of skill.

The tea master was horrified! What was he to do? He knew of this cruel samurai, how dangerous he was as a swordsman, and he knew that he would surely die for his folly. Feeling deep shame, the tea master returned to where he and the wise samurai were staying, carefully took off the armor, and woke the sleeping samurai. He told the samurai what he had done and, trembling, asked forgiveness for putting on the armor and for dishonoring the samurai's reputation. The wise and understanding samurai forgave the tea master, but told him sternly that he, the tea master, would have to meet the challenge and that the cruel samurai would surely kill him, either for not being an able swordsman or for pretending to be a samurai when he was not one.

The wise samurai then told the tea master to prepare a proper tea ceremony while he thought of a way for the tea master to defeat the cruel samurai. For those who do not know, a proper tea ceremony, to be performed skillfully, requires great preparation, concentration on details, and a focused discipline. The ceremony quickly calmed the tea master, revealing him to be truly the master of his art. The wise samurai was deeply moved by the skill and attention of the tea master while preparing the tea ceremony, and in this he discovered how the tea master would meet the challenge of the cruel samurai. He explained to the tea master that the secret to his success would be not in meeting the challenge as a samurai, but in facing the cruel samurai just as he is now, as the master of the tea ceremony.

So the next day at the appointed time the two met for the challenge. The cruel samurai was dressed in his finest battle armor. His appearance was very frightening. The tea master, on the other hand, wore his own ceremonial robe, carrying the wise samurai's armor. Immediately, without even acknowledging the other samurai, the tea master gently placed the armor aside and began the delicate preparation for a proper tea ceremony for the two of them.

The cruel samurai laughed at this sight, but quieted quickly, observing the skill, concentration and discipline of the master of the tea ceremony. Soon the cruel samurai himself became frightened as he thought how great this samurai must really be, and wondered, "If he prepares a simple tea ceremony with such skill and precision, how great a swordsman must he also be?" The cruel samurai, now thoroughly scared, prostrated himself on the ground, removed his sword, placing it at the feet of the tea master, and begged forgiveness and mercy for his arrogance.

The tea master, heaving a silent sigh of thankful relief, forgave the cruel samurai, who quickly left the city. The tea master then expressed his gratitude to the wise samurai for teaching him the secret of self-acceptance—know who you are, where you are and what you are doing.

23. Where Am I Going?

Anonymous

Supreme Court Justice Oliver Wendell Holmes had the reputation of being absent-minded. One day on a train out of Washington, Holmes was studying a pending case when the conductor asked for his ticket. The jurist searched each pocket nervously, but to no avail.

"Don't be concerned, Mr. Justice Holmes," the conductor said. "We know who you are. When you return to Washington, you can send us the ticket at your convenience."

Holmes lowered his eyes and shook his head sadly. "Thank you, my good man, but you don't seem to understand the problem. It's not a question of whether I'll pay the fare. The problem is: Where am I going?"

24. New Angles— A Fresh Outlook?

Anonymous

If you asked someone, "What's half of eight?" and received the answer, "zero," your first reaction would be, "That's nonsense."

But stop a moment! Think of the numeral 8. The figure is composed of two small 0's—zeros—one piled on top of another.

Take it further: If a line were drawn down the middle of 8, you would have two 3's standing face-to-face. From that perspective, half of 8 would be 3!

25. God Made Part of Me

Anonymous

"Can you tell me who made you?" the pastor asked the small boy.

The youngster thought a moment. Then he looked up at the pastor and said, "God made part of me."

"What do you mean, 'part of you?'" asked the pastor.

"Well," answered the boy, "God made me little. I grew the rest myself."

"Growing the rest" is a lifetime job for us all.

26. Make a Difference, #1

Anonymous

An old Jewish story tells of the reaction of a learned rabbi to this excited announcement by a member of his congregation: "The Messiah has come! He is in our city now!"

"Really," mused the rabbi. Going to the window, the rabbi looked out on the city and observed, "I see no difference."

Making a difference depends on us.

27. A Donkey, a Rooster and a Lamp

Anonymous

Rabbi Moshe took a trip to a strange land. He took a donkey, a rooster and a lamp. Since he was a Jew, he was refused hospitality in the village inns, so he decided to sleep in the woods.

He lit his lamp to study the holy books before going to sleep, but a fierce wind came up, knocking over the lamp and breaking it. The rabbi decided to turn in saying, "All that God does, he does well." During the night some wild animals came along and drove away the rooster, and thieves stole the donkey. Moshe woke up, saw the loss, but still proclaimed easily, "All that God does, he does well."

The rabbi then went back to the village where he was refused lodging, only to learn that enemy soldiers had invaded it during the night and killed all the inhabitants. He also learned that these soldiers had traveled through the same part of the woods where he lay asleep. Had his lamp not been broken, he would have been discovered. Had not the rooster been chased, it would have crowed, giving him away. Had not the donkey been stolen, it would have brayed. So once more Rabbi Moshe declared, "All that God does, he does well!"

28. Make a Difference, #2

Anonymous

As the old man walked the beach at dawn, he noticed a youth ahead of him picking up starfish and flinging them into the sea. Finally, catching up with the youth, he asked him why he was doing this. The answer was that the stranded starfish would die if left in the morning sun. "But the beach goes on for miles and there are millions of starfish," countered the old man. "How can your effort make any difference?"

The young man looked at the starfish in his hand, and then threw it to the safety of the waves. "It makes a difference to this one," he said.

29. The Magic Castle

Vernon Howard

Once upon a time a weary traveler was wandering down a dark and scary road. Suddenly there appeared before him a bright and marvelous castle with a welcome sign over the entrance. Knowing he had reached rest and safety at last, he felt glad.

Approaching the open gate, he saw a strange sight. Other lost travelers were walking right past the castle, as if it wasn't there. He asked a castle resident about this strange behavior and heard this reply: "This is a magic castle. It can be seen only by those who realize and admit they have lost their way. The castle can't appear to people who pretend to know where they are going, who demand their own way. Your own self-honesty made the castle appear to you. Enter, for all its riches are now yours."

30. Improve Gifts and Talents

Anonymous

Steve Garvey, the former first baseman for the San Diego Padres, was never cut from an athletic team in his schoolboy days. However, he was cut from the high school concert choir his senior year. His teacher told him he lacked the range needed for the school's first concert program of the season.

But Garvey was a determined young man. He practiced and practiced with a piano accompanist until he improved his voice quality. He later was part of the choir team that earned best-in-state at the Florida state championship.

31. On a Journey

Anonymous

You have been sent on a journey. You had no choice about when or where it started. You don't know when, where or how it will end. You have no map. All you know for sure is that it's bound to end sometime.

There are rules that apply to this journey, but you've had to learn them as you go. And you cannot control them. You may not even know the purpose of the journey, even though others claim to know.

All you know is that once started, you must continue every day, whether you feel like it or not. You start with no possessions, and when you finish you must turn in all you have accumulated.

In the end, say some, you will be rewarded or punished. But how do they know for sure?

That's life, my friends, and you cannot change it. A little faith and a sense of humor, fortunately, help cushion some of the bumps.

32. Obstacles?
…Deal with Them Now

Anonymous

An old farmer had plowed around a large rock in one of his fields for years. Several plowshares and a cultivator were broken on it, and he had grown rather tired of the rock.

After breaking yet another plowshare, and remembering all the trouble the rock had caused him through the years, he finally decided to do something about it. He'd had enough!

The farmer went to the shed to get some dynamite to blow the rock to smithereens. But when he put his pry bar under the rock, he was surprised that it lifted up so easily. Turns out that the rock, which had been such a huge obstacle all those years, was just a few inches thick, and that he could easily break it up with a sledgehammer.

As he was carting away the pieces, the farmer had to smile, remembering all the trouble that the rock had caused him over the years, and how easy it would have been to get rid of it sooner. What had seemed so huge an obstacle was actually quite smaller when he got a closer look at the problem.

33. The Face in the Window

Anonymous

It was Christmas eve. A jostling crowd of shoppers was busy grabbing last-minute bargains. A small girl in tattered clothes made her way through the crowd. Her name was Nelly. You will find such a girl in your city or town, if you will look around.

Nelly was also shopping—window shopping. She had no money and she was hungry. The twinkling lights, the colorful Christmas candles, the dazzling decorations and displays in the shop windows fascinated Nelly. As she passed the bakery with the cakes and pastries, she felt even more hungry. She paused…then moved a step closer to press her little snub nose against the window as she gazed at the Christmas "goodies." It lasted only a while. The manager saw her face in the window—the pale face pinched with hunger—so Nelly was told gruffly: "You there, be off!"

Nelly did not need a second bidding. She was frightened. She hurried through the crowd until she reached the attic where she lived with her aged grandma. Grandma was asleep. Sleep was the only thing they did not have to buy. This was the slumber that helped them forget misfortune—being hungry, no gifts, no new clothes, no decorations. Nelly also soon found refuge in sleep. From the distance wafted the strains of the well-loved carol, "Glory to God in the highest and peace on earth to men of good will."

Is there such a Nelly in your neighborhood with whom you can share the joys and blessings of Christmas? All you have to do is look around.

> We are charged to seek out those lost in the shuffle of
> life,
> to smooth out rough places;
> to fill in the valleys of hunger and want;
> to level out mountains of injustice.

We have been entrusted with the work of Advent—to make ready new heavens and a new earth. Look around; get to work!

34. My Crowd at Last

Anonymous

A man moved to a new city and started looking around for a church to join. He was about to give up finding just the right one until one Sunday he dropped into a church and heard the preacher say, "We have left undone the things we ought to have done, and we have done those things that we ought not to have done!"

The newcomer slipped into a pew, and with a sigh of relief said to himself, "Thank goodness! I've found my crowd at last."

35. I Created You!

Anonymous

One day, as usually was the case, a young waif, a little girl, stood at the street corner begging for food, money or whatever she could get. Now this girl was wearing very tattered clothes; she was dirty and quite disheveled.

As it happens, a well-to-do young man passed that corner without giving the girl a second look. But when he returned to his expensive home, his happy and comfortable family, and his well-laden dinner table, his thoughts returned to the young waif, and he became very angry at God for allowing such conditions to exist.

He reproached God, saying, "How can you let this happen? Why don't you do something to help this girl?"

Then he heard God in the depths of his being respond by saying, "I did. I created you!"

36. Peak Experience

Anonymous

It was an exhausting climb up the mountain. The sky was a vibrant shade of azure and the sun was shimmering hot. Sweat rippled down his back and trickled into his eyes. The baggage he carried increasingly became a hardship, until the weary seeker could not take another step in his quest to reach the peak. Overwhelmed, he put the baggage aside. The not-so-young man could climb no more.

After easing the baggage to the ground, he slumped against a tree, allowing a cool, refreshing breeze to waft over him. A bird in a nearby tree trilled softly. And, gazing upward, the seeker saw his goal, the mountain peak. Feeling renewed, he clambered to his feet to continue the journey.

With each steady stride the peak loomed closer; then, finally, he gained the summit. The panorama stretching out below was glorious. Spanning the horizon was a verdant valley interlaced with gurgling streams, sylvan glens and fertile meadows. Infused with the vision of a flourishing valley, the man scurried down from his peak experience and went to collect his belongings.

Placed alongside the trail were several boxes, a large backpack and an overstuffed briefcase. Picking up the first box he noticed that it contained his memories—awards, report cards, even a piece of an old flannel blanket. No longer sensing a need to rely on these memories, he put the box aside. And you know, he began to feel taller!

Next he opened the large backpack containing all the beauty he had collected along his journey—a piece of driftwood sculpture, photographs of rainbows and, of course, books. These, too, he put aside, remembering the beauty on the other side of the mountain. Again he felt a twinge of growth.

The briefcase was examined next. It was stuffed with various causes—those issues and concerns that had inflamed his spirit and impassioned past actions. However, these now seemed less significant. The overstuffed briefcase also was placed with the other discarded baggage. Now the not-so-young seeker felt more youthful, as well as taller!

Examining the remaining baggage, he discovered that most of it was no longer needed, save for a small backpack that he removed from the heap. The excess baggage he buried in a deep hole on the side of the mountain.

Now, aware of being rejuvenated, the seeker slung the small pack over his shoulder. It contained a hammer, a saw, some other tools and a bamboo flute. Once again the man ascended to the peak. He gazed back down the trail toward the resting place of the time-worn baggage he had carried for so long. Turning about, the seeker looked toward the valley below, realizing his journey had ended. With a spring in his step and a cool breeze at his back, the seeker grabbed his flute, and, while playing a merry tune, he walked into the valley of his future.

37. Grains of Caring

Anonymous

Two brothers worked together on the family farm. One was married and had a large family. The other was single. At the day's end, the brothers shared everything equally, produce and profit.

Then one day the single brother said to himself, "It's not right that we should share equally the produce and the profit. I'm alone and my needs are simple." So each night he took a sack of grain from his bin and crept across the field between their houses, dumping it into his brother's bin.

Meanwhile, the married brother said to himself, "It's not right that we should share the produce and the profit equally. After all, I'm married and I have my wife to look after me and my children for years to come. My brother has no one, and no one to take care of his future." So each night he, too, took a sack of grain and dumped it into his single brother's bin.

Both men were puzzled for years because their supply of grain never dwindled. Then one dark night, the two brothers bumped into each other. Slowly it dawned on them what was happening. They dropped their sacks and embraced one another.

38. Heaven and Hell

Anonymous

A man spoke with the Lord about heaven and hell. "I will show you hell," said the Lord, and they went into a room that had a large pot of stew in the middle. The smell was delicious, but around the pot sat desperate people who were starving. All were holding spoons with very long handles that reached into the pot, but because the handle of the spoon was longer than their arm, it was impossible to get the stew into their mouths. Their suffering was terrible.

"Now I will show you heaven," said the Lord, and they went into another room identical to the first one. There was a similar pot of delicious stew, and the people had the same long-handled spoons, but they were well-nourished, talking and happy. At first the man did not understand. "It is simple," said the Lord. "You see, they have learned to feed each other."

39. The Farmer and the Pumpkin

Earl Nightingale

One time there was a farmer who had planted a crop of pumpkins. Walking through his field when the pumpkins were just beginning to develop, he came across a glass jug, which apparently a passing motorist had thrown into his field. As an experiment, he poked a very small pumpkin through the mouth of the jug, but he was careful not to damage the vine.

Months later, when the field was fully developed and about ready for harvesting, the farmer, making one of his periodic inspections, again came across the glass jug. This time it was completely filled with the pumpkin he had put inside. The other pumpkins on the same vine were large and fully developed, but the pumpkin in the jug had not been able to grow beyond the confines of the glass prison and was shaped to its exact dimensions.

What size and kind of jug are you going to poke yourself into or allow someone else to poke you into?

40. Attention...

Anonymous

One day a leader of the people asked Zen Master Ikkyu: "Master, will you please write for me some maxims of the highest wisdom?"

Ikkyu immediately took his brush and wrote the word "Attention."

"Is that all?" asked the leader. "Will you not add something more?"

Ikkyu then wrote twice: "Attention...Attention."

"Well," remarked the leader rather irritably, "I really don't see much depth or subtlety in what you have just written."

Then Ikkyu wrote the same word three times: "Attention...Attention...Attention."

Half-angered, the leader demanded, "What does that word 'Attention' mean anyway?"

And Ikkyu answered gently, "'Attention' means attention."

41. So Wise

Anonymous

An old country doctor was celebrated for his wisdom. "Dr. Sage," a young man asked, "how did you get so wise?"

"Weren't hard," said the doc, "I've got good judgment."

"Well, Doc, how does one get good judgment?"

"That's easy," said Doc Sage. "Good judgment comes from experience. And experience—well, that comes from having bad judgment."

42. Always Be Alert

Anonymous

Waiting in a steamship office to be interviewed for a job as a wireless operator, a group of applicants filled the room with such a buzz of conversation that they were oblivious to the dots and dashes that began coming over a loudspeaker.

About that time another man entered and sat down quietly by himself. Suddenly he snapped to attention, walked into the private office, and a few minutes later came out smiling with a new job.

"Say," one of the group called out, "how'd you get in ahead of us? We were here first."

"One of you would have gotten the job," the successful applicant replied, "if you had listened to the message from the loudspeaker."

"What message?" they asked in surprise.

"Why, the code," the man answered. "It said: 'The man I need must always be on the alert. The first one who gets this message and comes directly into my private office will be placed on one of my ships as operator.'"

43. Fact, Faith and Feeling

Anonymous

Three companions—Mr. Fact, Mr. Faith and Mr. Feeling—were walking along, one in front of the other, on top of a wall. Suddenly Mr. Feeling, who was last in line, and who was not noted for his good balance, stumbled and fell from the wall. He reached out and grasped Mr. Faith, who also slipped and fell from the wall. Fortunately, Mr. Fact had a good grasp of the situation. He was not moved easily and stood firm as a rock. By doing so, he was able to help Mr. Faith to get back up. At last, between Mr. Fact and Mr. Faith, they were able to restore a shaken Mr. Feeling back up on the wall and to continue their journey, though Mr. Feeling was quite unsteady.

44. Three Questions

Anonymous

In one of the scenes from the play *1776*, the stage curtain opens. An actor is heard walking onto the darkly lighted set, and he directs three questions out of the shadows toward the audience:

1. Is anyone there?
2. Is anyone listening?
3. Does anyone care?

The curtain closes and we hear the retreating footsteps of the actor.

45. The Moso Bamboo

Joel Weldon

The moso is a bamboo plant that grows in China and the Far East. After the moso is planted, no visible growth occurs for up to five years—even under ideal conditions!

Then, as if by magic, it suddenly begins growing at the rate of nearly two and one half feet per day, reaching a full height of ninety feet within six weeks.

But it's not magic. The moso's rapid growth is due to the miles of roots it develops during those first five years, five years of getting ready.

46. Attitude at Work

Anonymous

Back in the Middle Ages, a dispatcher went out to determine how laborers felt about their work. He went to a building site in France.

He approached the first worker and asked, "What are you doing?"

"What, are you blind?" the worker snapped back. "I'm cutting these impossible boulders with primitive tools and putting them together the way the boss tells me. I'm sweating under this blazing sun, it's back-breaking work and it's boring me to death."

The dispatcher quickly backed off and retreated to a second worker. He asked the same question, "What are you doing?"

The worker replied, "I'm shaping these boulders into usable forms, which are then assembled according to the architect's plans. It's hard work and sometimes it gets repetitive, but I earn five francs a week and that supports the wife and kids. It's a job. Could be worse, too."

Somewhat encouraged, the dispatcher went on to a third worker. "And what are you doing?" he asked.

"Why, can't you see?" said the worker as he lifted his arm to the sky, "I'm building a cathedral!"

Now that's the joy of working.

47. Light Too Bright

Anonymous

There was a young man whose search for God led him to seek out a wise spiritual director. The lad was told to quit his dissolute life, pray in earnest and purify his motives. Sick of his sinful history, the youth made steady improvement and, slowly, health, courage and joy returned.

The spiritual director went away for a while, leaving the young man on his own. When the spiritual director returned, he sought out his promising protégé and asked, "How's it going?" The youth's face clouded over. He admitted to having given up all his prayerful practices, and of slipping back into his old negative habits.

"But why? What happened?" asked the puzzled spiritual director.

"I opened the door," the boy answered sadly, "and found the light was too bright."

48. Eagle...or Prairie Chicken?

Anonymous

There's an American Indian tale about a young brave who found an eagle's egg and put it into the nest of a prairie chicken. The eaglet hatched with the brood of chicks and grew up with them.

All its life the changeling eagle, thinking it was a prairie chicken, did what the other prairie chickens did. It scratched in the dirt for seeds and insects to eat. It clucked and cackled. And it flew in a brief thrashing of wings and flurry of feathers no more than a few feet off the ground. After all, that's how prairie chickens were supposed to fly.

Years passed, and the changeling eagle grew bigger and stronger. One day, it saw a magnificent bird soaring far above in the cloudless sky. Hanging with graceful majesty on the powerful wind currents, it soared with scarcely a beat of its strong, golden wings.

"What a beautiful bird!" said the changeling eagle to its neighbor, an old prairie chicken. "What is it?"

"That's an eagle—the chief of the birds," the neighbor cackled. "But don't you give it a second thought. You could never be like him. You're only a prairie chicken."

So the changeling eagle never gave it another thought. And it died always thinking it was a prairie chicken.

49. Take Action

Anonymous

A pastor once made an investment in a large piece of ranch real estate, which he hoped to enjoy during his retirement years. While he was still an active pastor, he would take one day off each

37

week to go out to his land and work. But what a job! What he had bought, he soon realized, was several acres of weeds, gopher holes and run-down buildings. It was anything but attractive, but the pastor knew it had potential and he stuck with it.

Every week he'd go to his ranch, crank up his small tractor and plow through the weeds with vengeance. Then he'd spend time doing repairs on the buildings. He'd mix cement, cut lumber, replace broken windows and work on the plumbing. It was hard work, but after several months the place began to take shape. And every time the pastor put his hand to some task, he would swell with pride. He knew his labor was finally paying off.

When the project was completed, the pastor received a neighborly visit from a farmer who lived a few miles down the road. Farmer Brown took a long look at the preacher and cast a longer eye over the revitalized property. Then he nodded his approval and said, "Well, preacher, it looks like you and God really did some work here."

The pastor, wiping the sweat from his face, answered, "It's interesting you should say that, Mr. Brown, but I've got to tell you something. You should have seen this place when God had it all to himself."

50. Heroes

Anonymous

Babe Ruth had hit 714 home runs during his baseball career and was playing one of his last full major league games. It was the Braves versus the Reds in Cincinnati. But the great Bambino was no longer as agile as he had been. He fumbled the ball and threw badly, and in one inning alone his errors were responsible for most of the five runs scored by Cincinnati.

As the Babe walked off the field and headed toward the dugout after the third out, a crescendo of yelling and booing reached his ears. Just then a boy jumped over the railing onto the playing field. With tears streaming down his face, he threw his arms around the legs of his hero.

Ruth didn't hesitate for a second. He picked up the boy, hugged him and set him down on his feet, patting his head gently. The noise from the stands came to an abrupt halt. Suddenly, there was no more booing. In fact, a hush fell over the entire park. In those brief moments, the fans saw two heroes: Ruth, who, in spite of his dismal day on the field, could still care about a little boy; and the small lad, who cared about the feelings of another human being. Both had melted the hearts of the crowd.

51. Brother Jeremiah and Christian Service

Anonymous

If I had my life to live over again, I'd try to make more mistakes next time. I would relax. I would limber up. I would be sillier than I have been this trip. I know of very few things I would take seriously. I would take more vacations. I would climb more mountains, swim more rivers and watch more sunsets. I would do more walking and looking. I would eat more ice cream and less beans. I would have more actual troubles and fewer imaginary ones.

You see, I am one of those people who live preventively and sensibly and sanely, hour after hour, day after day. Oh, I've had my moments, and if I had to do it over again, I'd have more of them. In fact, I'd try to have nothing else. Just moments, one after another, instead of living so many years ahead each day. I have been one of those people who never goes anywhere without a thermometer, a hot water bottle, a raincoat, aspirin and a parachute. If I had it to do over again, I would go places, do things and travel lighter than I have.

If I had my life to live over, I would start barefooted earlier in the spring and stay that way later in the fall. I would play more. I would ride on more merry-go-rounds. I'd pick more daisies.

52. Prayer Methods

Anonymous

The disciple asks his master, "What can I do to attain God?"

The master answers by asking, "What can you do to make the sun rise?"

The disciple says indignantly, "Then why are you giving us all these methods of prayer?"

And the master replies, "To make sure you're awake when the sun rises."

53. Encouragement

Anonymous

Dante Gabriel Rossetti, the famous nineteenth-century poet and artist, was once approached by an elderly man. The old fellow had some sketches and drawings that he wanted Rossetti to look at and tell him if they were any good, or if they at least showed potential talent.

Rossetti looked them over carefully. After the first few he knew that they were worthless, showing not the least sign of artistic talent. But Rossetti was a kind man, and he told the elderly man as gently as possible that the pictures were without much value and showed little talent. He was sorry, but he could not lie to the man.

The visitor was disappointed, but seemed to expect Rossetti's judgment. He then apologized for taking up Rossetti's time, but would he just look at a few more drawings—ones done by a young art student?

Rossetti looked over the second batch of sketches and immediately enthused over the talent they revealed. "These," he said, "oh, these are good. This young student has great talent. He should be given every help and encouragement in his career as an artist. He has a great future, if he will work hard and stick to it."

Rossetti could see that the old fellow was deeply moved. "Who is this fine young artist?" he asked. "Your son?"

"No," said the old man sadly. "It is me, forty years ago. If only I heard your praise then! For you see, I got discouraged and gave up—too soon."

54. Merchant of Death

Anonymous

About eighty years ago a man picked up the morning paper and, to his horror, read his own obituary! The newspaper had reported the death of the wrong man. Like most of us, he relished the idea of finding out what people would say about him after he died. He read past the bold caption that stated, "Dynamite King dies," to the text itself. He read along until he was taken aback by the description of him as a "merchant of death."

He was the inventor of dynamite, and he had amassed a great fortune from the manufacture of weapons of destruction. But he was moved by this description. Did he really want to be known as a "merchant of death"?

It was at that moment that a healing power greater than the destructive force of dynamite came over him. It was his hour of conversion. From that point on, he devoted his energy and money to works of peace and human betterment. Today, of course, he is best remembered not as a "merchant of death," but as the founder of the Nobel Peace Prize—Alfred Nobel.

55. Tell Them, Now

Anonymous

A charming old gentleman used to stop by occasionally at an antique shop in New Hampshire to sell furniture. One day after he left, the antique dealer's wife said that she wished she had told him how much she enjoyed his visits. The husband said, "Next time let's tell him so."

The following summer a young woman came in and introduced herself as the daughter of the old gentleman. Her father, she said, had died. Then the wife told her about the conversation she and her husband had had after the old gentleman's last visit. The young woman's eyes filled with tears. "Oh, how much good that would have done my father!" she cried. "He was a man who needed to be reassured that he was liked."

"Since that day," the shopkeeper said later, "whenever I think something particularly nice about people, I tell them. I might never get another chance."

56. The Lowly Paper Clip

Anonymous

Several years ago an expensive laboratory jet was approaching Edwards Air Force Base in California. When the pilot tried to lower the nose gear to landing position, it didn't respond.

The co-pilot ran a quick check and traced the problem to a faulty relay panel. Recognizing the problem, he hunted around for something to bypass the relay and activate the nose gear.

He found a paper clip and bent it so that it bypassed the problem and triggered the nose gear. It worked like a charm, saving the expensive jet from a crash landing.

At that moment, for that special job, the lowly paper clip was more important than the rest of the sophisticated equipment on the plane.

57. Attitude Changes Everything

Anonymous

There was a poor widow who had two sons. This widow's livelihood depended entirely upon her sons' meager little businesses because she was so weak and frail. Every day she worried about their businesses. She fretted and hoped that they would do well.

One son sold umbrellas. So the mother would waken in the morning and the first thing she would look for was to see if the sun was shining or if it looked like rain. If it was dark and cloudy out she would gleefully say, "Oh, he will surely sell umbrellas today!" But if the sun was shining, she would be miserable all day because she feared that nobody would buy her son's umbrellas.

The widow's other son sold fans. Every morning the poor old widow would arise and look to the skies. If the sun was hidden and it looked like a rainy day, she would get very depressed and moan, "Nobody's going to buy my son's fans today."

No matter what the weather was, this poor old widow had something to fret about. If the sun was shining, she felt terrible because nobody would buy her son's umbrellas. If the sun was not shining and it was cloudy, she also felt terrible, because nobody would buy her son's fans. With such an attitude she was bound to lose.

One day she ran into a friend who said, "Why, you've got it all wrong, my dear. There's no way you can lose. If the sun is shining, people will buy fans; if it rains, they'll buy umbrellas. You live off both of your sons. You cannot lose!"

When that simple, obvious, consciousness gripped her

mood, she changed. From then on, according to the story, she was a happy woman the rest of her life.

58. Find Someone in Need

Anonymous

Dr. Karl Menninger, the famous psychiatrist, once gave a lecture on mental health, and then answered questions from the audience. "What would you advise a person to do," asked one man, "if that person felt a nervous breakdown coming on?"

Most people expected him to reply, "Consult a psychiatrist." To their astonishment, he replied, "Lock up your house, go across the railway tracks, find someone in need and do something to help that person."

MORAL: Don't sit and pout. Get up and do something!

59. Opportunity

Anonymous

In the days before modern harbors, a ship had to wait for the flood tide before it could make it to port. The term for this situation in Latin was *ob portu,* that is, a ship standing over against port, waiting for the moment when it could ride the turn of the tide to harbor.

The English word *opportunity* is derived from this original meaning. The captain and the crew were ready and waiting for that one moment, for they knew that if they missed it, they would have to wait for another tide to come in. Shakespeare turned this background of the exact meaning of opportunity into one of his most famous passages:

There is a tide in the affairs of men,
Which, taken at the flood, leads on to fortune;
Omitted, all the voyage of their life
Is bound in shallows and in miseries.
On such a full sea are we now afloat;
And we must take the current when it serves,
Or lose our ventures.

60. Growing Older

Anonymous

When the poet Henry Wadsworth Longfellow was well along in years, his hair was white, but he was still a vigorous man. Someone asked him why this was so.

The poet pointed to an apple tree in bloom and said, "That tree is very old, but I never saw prettier blossoms on it than it now bears. That tree grows new wood each year. Like that apple tree, I try to grow a little new wood each year."

61. Where to Hide God?

Anonymous

Once there were three wise men who were given the task of hiding God so well that no one would ever find him again. They sat down around a council table to ponder the possibilities.

The first wise man said that God should be hidden on the farthest star. But the second wise man feared that rocket ships would one day reach that star and God would be discovered. "Let's put God at the bottom of the deepest ocean," he said. The third wise man thought for a time. Finally he spoke, saying that he could foresee the day when food would be grown on the ocean's floor to feed the world, and God would be found.

So this wise man said, "The only place we can hide God so that no one will ever find him again is inside each person. No one will discover God there."

62. Remember, You Must Die

Anonymous

There is a novel by Muriel Spark called *Memento Mori*. It tells about a group of friends, all over sixty-five, who one by one receive anonymous phone calls telling them, "Remember, you must die!"

The novel, partly serious, partly humorous, tells how different individuals come to terms with the telephone message. Though reactions vary, a common reaction is fright.

Still, the anonymous caller often causes characters to think back over their lives and assess how they have lived—about the good they have done as well as the not-so-good. In a way, the message they receive about death forces them to come to terms with the meaning of the life they have lived. Somehow death leads them back into life.

63. Legend of the Trees

Anonymous

Why are only certain trees green during the winter?

It seems that many, many years ago, Manitou, the Great Spirit, allowed all things to roam freely on the face of the Earth. Even as the elk and bear, deer, the fox and humans could move from place to place, the trees could move, too. They could seek water, the warmth of the sun, and shade in the shadow of a hill when the heat was too intense.

They did not move quickly like the deer or the rabbit, of course. They would move slowly and ponderously—the giant elm, the poplar, the mighty oak and the hickory. They would roam the valleys and hillsides during the spring, summer and the fall, then rest for the winter to await the coming of a new spring.

There came a time when these giants of the forest quarreled among themselves. One was jealous of the other. The elm wanted the hillside; the poplar wanted the valley where the oak was. The hickory wanted to be near the stream where the beech stood. Only the pines and firs seemed satisfied not to quarrel. They were small trees, and because they had long, pointy shaped needles for leaves, were not welcomed by the other trees.

The Great Spirit heard the crashing of the trees in the forest. With a great thunderclap he shouted for them to stop. "I have given you life and the beauty of your leaves and fruit, and the ability to roam the Earth, and you are not satisfied!"

There was another thunderclap as he spoke. "From this day on, you will be rooted in the ground and not be able to move freely on the Earth. Only your seeds will be able to roam. You will lose your leaves when the cold and snow and ice come, and shall shiver in the forests until the spring, because you were not satisfied with what I had given you. Only the gentle pine, cedar, spruce and fir shall keep their tiny green leaves throughout the year and be called evergreens. They will grow tall and straight, and they will be the ones who shall hold their heads above all the other trees in the forest."

And so it came to pass many years ago. To this day, while walking through a forest in the winter, you can hear the moaning of the trees that have lost their leaves and shiver in the cold, waiting for the spring.

64. Handling Criticism

Anonymous

Once there was a politician who did the best job he could. But being human, he made mistakes and was criticized. Reporters wrote about his errors in the newspaper. Well, he became so upset that he drove out into the country to visit his dear friend, a farmer. "What am I going to do?" the politician asked. "I've tried so hard. Nobody has tried harder than I have to do more good for more people, and look how they criticize me!"

But the old farmer could hardly hear the complaint of his persecuted politician friend because his hound dog was barking up a storm at the full moon. The farmer rebuked his dog, but the dog kept barking. Finally, the farmer said to the politician, "Do you want to know how you should handle your unfair critics? Here's how. Listen to that dog; now, look up at the moon. And remember that people will keep yelling at you. They'll nip at your heels, and they'll criticize you. But here's the lesson: *The dog keeps howling, but the moon keeps shining!*"

65. Diagnosing…Check the Size

Anonymous

A man was bothered with continual ringing in his ears, bulging eyes and a flushed face. Over a period of three years, he went to one doctor after another. One took out his tonsils, one removed his appendix, another pulled all his teeth. He even tried a goat-gland treatment in Switzerland—all to no avail. Finally, one doctor told him there was no hope; he had six months to live.

The poor fellow quit his job, sold all his belongings and decided to live it up in the time he had left. He went to his tailor and ordered several suits and shirts. The tailor measured his neck and wrote down "16$^{1}/_{2}$."

The man corrected him. "It's 15$^{1}/_{2}$," he said.

The tailor measured again: 16$^{1}/_{2}$.

But the man insisted that he'd always worn a size 15$^{1}/_{2}$.

"Well, all right," said the tailor. "Just don't come back here complaining if you have ringing ears, bulging eyes and a flushed face!"

66. Essence of Tact

Anonymous

A sultan called in one of his seers and asked how long he would live. "Sire," said the seer, "you will live to see all your sons dead." The sultan flew into a rage and handed the prophet over to his guards for execution.

He then called for a second seer and asked him the same question. "Sire," said the prophet, "I see you blessed with long life, so long that you will outlive all your family." The sultan was delighted and rewarded this seer with gold and silver jewelry.

Both prophets knew the truth, but one had tact, the other did not.

67. No Talent

Anonymous

A young free-lance artist tried to sell his sketches to a number of newspapers. They all turned him down. One Kansas City editor told him he had no talent.

But he had faith in his ability and kept trying to sell his work. Finally, he got a job making drawings for church publicity material. He rented a mouse-infested garage to turn out his sketches, and he continued to produce free-lance drawings in hope that someone would buy them.

One of the mice in the garage must have inspired him, for he created a cartoon character called Mickey Mouse. Walt Disney was on his way.

68. How to Get to Heaven

Anonymous

The Reverend Billy Graham tells of a time early in his ministry when he arrived in a small town to preach a sermon. Wanting to mail a letter, he asked a young boy where the post office was. When the boy had told him, Dr. Graham thanked him and said, "If you'll come to the Baptist church this evening, you can hear me telling everyone how to get to heaven."

"I don't think I'll be there," the boy said. "You don't even know your way to the post office."

69. Now That's Motivation

Zig Ziglar

There was this very rich, good old Texan who threw a big Texas bash for his daughter. Now he was a very rich Texan with tens of thousands of acres of land, thousands of cattle, hundreds of producing oil wells, a large twenty-nine room mansion with a swimming pool, and a beautiful young daughter.

For this party he invited all the eligible young men of the county to meet his daughter. After the party had been going on for some time, he called everyone out to the pool for an announcement. He lined all the young men at one end of the

Olympic-sized pool, which he had filled with snakes and alligators, and said, "The first one of you who jumps into the pool and swims to the other end, I will give him the choice of one million dollars, a thousand acres of choice land, or the hand of my daughter in marriage."

No sooner were the words out of the Texan's mouth when there was a splash at the far end and a streak through the water. A young man emerged, setting what must have equaled an Olympic record.

The Texan approached the young man and asked if he wanted the million dollars? The man said, "No, sir." Then he was asked if he wanted the thousand acres. Again the young man said, "No, sir."

"Well then, son," said the Texan, "you must want the hand of my lovely daughter in marriage?"

"Thank you, but no, sir," replied the young man.

"Well then, just what is it that you do want?"

"What I want, sir, is to know the name of the dude who pushed me in the pool!"

70. Balance

Anonymous

Once the great St. Anthony of the Desert was relaxing with his disciples outside his hut when a hunter came by. The hunter was surprised to see Anthony relaxing, and rebuffed him for taking it easy. It was not his idea of what a holy monk should be doing.

Anthony replied, "Bend your bow and shoot an arrow." And the hunter did so. "Bend it again and shoot another arrow," said Anthony. The hunter did so, again and again.

The hunter finally said, "Abba Anthony, if I keep my bow always stretched, it will break."

"So it is with the monk," replied Anthony. "If we push ourselves beyond measure, we will break. It is right from time to time to relax our efforts."

71. How We Look at Things

Anonymous

There is the story of identical twins. One was a hope-filled optimist: "Everything is coming up roses!" he would say. The other twin was a sad and hopeless pessimist. He was sure that Murphy, as in "Murphy's Law," was an optimist. The worried parents of the boys brought them to the local psychologist.

He suggested to the parents a plan to balance their personalities. "On their next birthday, put them in separate rooms to open their gifts. Give the pessimist the best toys you can afford, and give the optimist a box of manure." The parents followed these instructions and carefully observed the results.

When they peeked in on the pessimist, they heard him audibly complaining, "I don't like the color of this computer...I'll bet this calculator will break...I don't like the game...I know someone who's got a bigger toy car than this...."

Tiptoeing across the corridor, the parents peeked in and saw their little optimist gleefully throwing the manure up in the air. He was giggling, "You can't fool me! Where there's this much manure, there's gotta be a pony!"

72. Learn from Mistakes

Anonymous

Thomas Edison tried over two thousand different materials in search of a filament for the light bulb. When none worked satisfactorily, his assistant complained, "All our work is in vain. We have learned nothing."

Edison replied very confidently, "Oh, we have come a long way, and we have learned a lot. We now know that there are more than two thousand elements that we cannot use to make a good light bulb filament."

73. Notice and Observe Others

Anonymous

Once a wise old botany teacher was speaking to a group of young and eager students. He gave them an assignment to go out by the side of some lonely road and find a small, unnoticed flower. He asked them to study the flower for a long time. "Get a magnifying glass and study the delicate veins in the leaves, and notice the nuances and shades of color. Turn the leaf slowly and observe its symmetry. And remember: this flower might have gone unnoticed and unappreciated if you had not found and admired it," he told his students.

When the class returned after carrying out the assignment, the wise old teacher observed: "People are just like that unnoticed flower, too. Each one is different, carefully crafted, uniquely endowed. But you have to spend time with a person to realize this. So many people go unnoticed and unappreciated because no one has ever taken time with them and admired their uniqueness."

74. On Being a Saint

Anonymous

Once upon a time, long, long ago, a young man decided to become a saint. He left his home, family and possessions. He said goodbye to relatives and friends, sold all he owned, gave the money to the poor and walked off into the desert to find God.

He walked through the desert sands until he found a dark cave. "Here," he thought, "I will be alone with God. Here nothing can distract me from God." He prayed day and night in the dark cave. But God sent him great temptations. He imagined all the good things of life and wanted them desperately. However, he was determined to give up everything in order to have God alone. After many months the temptations stopped. St. Anthony of the Desert was at peace having nothing but God.

But then, according to legend, God said, "Leave your cave for a few days and go off to a distant town. Look for the town shoemaker. Knock on his door and stay with him a while."

The holy hermit was puzzled by God's command, but left the next morning. He walked all day across the desert sands. By nightfall he came to the village, found the home of the shoemaker and knocked on the door. A smiling man opened the door.

"Are you the town shoemaker?" the hermit asked.

"Yes, I am," the shoemaker answered. He noticed how tired and hungry the hermit looked. "Come in," he said. "You need something to eat and a place to rest." The shoemaker called his wife. They prepared a fine meal for the hermit and gave him a good bed to sleep in.

The hermit stayed with the shoemaker and his family for three days. The hermit asked many questions about their lives. But he didn't tell them much about himself, even though the couple were very curious about his life in the desert. They talked a lot and became good friends.

Then the hermit said goodbye to the shoemaker and his wife. He walked back to his cave wondering why God had sent him to visit the shoemaker.

"What was the shoemaker like?" God asked the hermit when he settled down again in his dark cave.

"He is a simple man," the hermit began. "He has a wife who is going to have a baby. They seem to love each other very much. He has a small shop where he makes shoes. He works hard. They have a simple house. They give money and food to those who have less than they have. He and his wife believe very strongly in you and pray at least once a day. They have many friends. And the shoemaker enjoys telling jokes."

God listened carefully. "You are a great saint, Anthony," God said, "and the shoemaker and his wife are great saints, too."

75. On Heaven

Anonymous

There is a story of a woman who had been used to every luxury and to all respect. She died, and when she arrived in heaven, an angel was sent to conduct her to her house there. They passed many a lovely mansion, and the woman thought that each one, as they came to it, must be the one allotted to her. When they had passed through the main streets, they came to the out-skirts where the houses were much smaller; on the very fringe they came to one that was little more than a shack.

"That is your house," said the conducting angel.

"What!" said the woman. "That! I cannot live in that."

"I am sorry," said the angel, "but that is all we could build for you with the materials you sent up."

76. The Ten Commandments

Anonymous

"Before I die I mean to make a pilgrimage to the Holy Land," a nineteenth-century industrial baron once said to Mark Twain. "I will climb to the top of Mount Sinai and read the Ten Commandments aloud."

"Why don't you stay home and keep them?" replied Twain.

77. Sadness in Beauty

Anonymous

The old man with the bent shoulders came out of the rain, furling his rice-paper umbrella as if it were a ship's sail. With some deliberation, he climbed the slate step and crept past the carved stone pot into which clear water flowed from a cut length of bamboo just above.

There he paused a moment, cocking his head like the most attentive of pupils, listening to the confluence of sounds: the pitter-patter of the rain at his back, the cheery gurgle of the flowing water at his side. There was within that mingling, he thought, the precise mix of the melancholy and the joyous that made life so exquisite to live. "There is sadness in beauty," he recalled his father telling him as a child. "When you can understand that, you will no longer be a boy."

78. Loneliness

Anonymous

Last year a man died. We'll call him Ben, though his name doesn't really matter. In one form or another, we have all known Ben, and we have all been Ben. Ben was seventy-six years old and had been a widower for two years. He was alert, intelligent, healthy and desperately unhappy.

In the spring Ben took a nasty fall. Though the doctors had not felt the injuries were that serious, three days later he was dead. A conclusion that was reached by a number of people who knew Ben was that he had quit living; he chose no longer to cling to hope. Ben didn't die from a fall; he died of acute loneliness. Ben had no will to live because his life had become a succession of days that were all yawningly empty.

But perhaps the saddest part of Ben's story is that he also chose loneliness. After the death of his wife, his family and friends tried constantly to get him out and get him involved. He was invited on trips, he was invited to join clubs, he was invited to dinners. "I don't want to have anything to do with those crippled old fools," is the way Ben would explain his latest rejection. And yet, in the next breath, he'd be lamenting his loneliness. Ben's prison of isolation was erected, brick by brick, with his own hand.

79. Be a Flame

Aesop

Once upon a time there was a piece of iron that was very strong. One after another, the ax, the saw, the hammer and the flame tried to break it.

"I'll master it," said the ax. Its blows fell heavily on the iron, but every blow made its edge more blunt, until it ceased to strike.

"Leave it to me," said the saw, and it worked backward and forward on the iron's surface until its jagged teeth were all worn and broken. Then it fell aside.

"Ah!" said the hammer. "I knew you wouldn't succeed. I'll show you the way." But at the first fierce blow, off flew its head, and the iron remained as before.

"Shall I try?" asked the small, soft flame?

"Forget it," all replied. "What can you do?"

But the flame curled around the iron, embraced it, and never left the iron until it melted under the flame's irresistible influence.

And you? Do you pound and try to break through? Or are you a steady flame that melts a breakthrough?

80. Three Sons with Special Talents

William J. Bausch

There was once a village chief with three sons. Each one had a special talent. The oldest son had the talent for raising olive trees, and would trade the oil for tools and cloth. The second son was a shepherd, and when the sheep were ill he had a great talent for making them well again. The third son was a dancer. When there was a streak of bad luck in the family, or when everyone was bored during the hard winters and were tired of work, this was the son who would cheer them up with his dancing.

One day the father had to go away on a long journey. He called his sons together and said, "My sons, the villagers are depending on you. Each of you has a special talent for helping people, and so, while I'm gone, see to it that you use your talents as wisely and well as possible, so that when I return I will find our village even more happy and prosperous than it is now." He embraced his sons and departed.

For a while things went well. Then the cold winter winds began to blow and the blizzards and snow came. First, the buds on the olive trees shrank and cracked, and it was a long time before the trees would recover. Then the village, because of the especially long winter, ran out of firewood. Desperate, the villagers began to cut down the olive trees, but in the process they were destroying part of the village.

In addition, the snow and ice made it impossible for traders to come up the river, or over the pass. The result was that the villagers murmured, "Let's kill and eat the sheep so we don't starve to death." The second son refused for a time, but finally had to give in to the hungry villagers. He remarked, "What good would it be to spare the sheep only to have the villagers perish?"

In this way, the villagers received just enough wood for their fires and food for their tables. However, the bitter winter had broken their spirits and they began to think that things were really worse than they were. They even began to lose hope—so much so that, family by family, they deserted the village in search of a more hospitable environment.

As spring began to loosen the icy grip of winter, the village chief, the father of the three sons, returned to find smoke rising only from his own chimney. "What have you done?" he stammered upon reaching his house and seeing his sons. "What has happened to the villagers?"

"Oh, Father, forgive me," cried the eldest son. "Our people were freezing and begged me to cut down the olive trees for firewood, and so I did. I gave away my talent. I am no longer fit to be an orchard keeper."

"Don't be angry, Father," said the second son. "The sheep would have frozen to death anyway, and the people were starving. I had to send my flock to the slaughter."

The father understood their sacrifices and replied, "Don't be ashamed, my sons. You did the best you could and you acted rightly and humanely. You used your talents wisely in trying to save our people. But, tell me, what has become of them? Where are they?"

The two brothers looked with eyes fixed on the third son who said, "Welcome home, Father. Yes, it has been a hard time. There was so little to eat and so little firewood. I thought that it would be insensitive and improper to dance during the sufferings, and, besides, I needed to conserve my strength so that I could dance for you when you came home."

"Then, dance, my son," groaned the father, "for my village is empty and so is my heart. Fill it with joy and courage once again. Yes, please dance!"

But as the third son went to get up, he made a face of pain and fell down. His legs were so stiff and sore from sitting that they were no longer fit for dancing.

The father was so sad that he could not even be angry. He simply said to the third son, "Ours was a strong village. It could have survived the want of fuel and food, but it could never survive without hope. Because you failed to use your talent wisely and well, our people gave up what little hope they had left. Now what? The village is deserted and you are crippled. Your punishment has already fallen upon you."

81. Make Life an Adventure

Roger Dawson

Fred Spencer wrote a popular book named *The Jungle Is Neutral*. Spencer had been a soldier in World War II, stationed in a small garrison on the island of Singapore, just off the tip of the Malay Peninsula. The British defense of this garrison was rather one-sided, as they felt that no army could ever pass through the impenetrable jungles to the north, and that any attack on Singapore would have to come from the sea.

To the chagrin of the British, however, the Japanese did the seemingly impossible and passed through the thick jungles of the peninsula to attack the garrison from the north. Singapore fell almost without a fight.

Spencer, though, was able to escape into the jungle, and he spent nine months there before he was able to rejoin his countrymen.

He had heard two conflicting reports about the jungle, however, and so at the time of his flight, he really had very little idea of what to expect. He had heard that the jungle was a horrible place filled with snakes and insects, fruit so poisonous that one bite would kill, and brutal wild animals. Therefore, any man lost in the harsh forests would die very quickly. But the other story Spencer had been told was that the jungle was a lush, tropical paradise with plenty of fresh water and edible fruit. In other words, it was a place where anyone could survive with relative ease.

The truth that Spencer discovered during his nine months in that jungle was that it is neutral. Spencer found that the jungle was neither pre-set to destroy him by making it impossible to survive, nor was it structured to support him. He learned that his survival depended directly on the amount of effort he put forth to survive. Spencer was able to make of his environment what he chose it to be.

Is life a jungle? Life, too, is neutral!

82. Follower...or Disciple?

Anonymous

Two learned professors were discussing the great thoughts on wisdom and the meaning of life.

The first professor asked the second, "Henry tells me he is one of your students."

The second professor replied, "Well, Henry does attend most of my classes, but certainly he is not one of my students."

Too bad there are so many distant followers and so few real disciples.

83. God Is Within You

Anonymous

A little girl was standing with her grandfather by an old-fashioned open well. They had just lowered a bucket and had drawn some water to drink.

"Grandfather," asked the little girl, "where does God live?"

The old man picked up his little granddaughter and held her over the open well. "Look down into the well," he said, "and tell me what you see."

"I see a reflection of myself," said the little girl.

"That's where God lives," said the grandfather. "He lives in you."

84. Kudzu—Wonder or Menace?

Anonymous

Kudzu, says *The Columbia Encyclopedia*, has large purple flowers. In the Orient, it is cultivated for its edible tubers and for its hemplike fiber. In 1876, it was brought to America from Japan for use as a decoration at the Japanese pavilion at the Centennial Exposition in Philadelphia.

In the early 1900s a Florida farmer, C. E. Pleas, became what might be called the apostle of kudzu after growing the plant as a flower. It spread rapidly, and when his livestock took a liking to the leaves, Pleas began to market the harvested plant leaves as fodder and to offer root stock by mail order.

In the 1930s, the U.S. government "discovered" kudzu, seeing in it an effective deterrent to soil erosion. So it was that the government distributed some 84 million seedlings in the southeast between 1935 and 1942. By 1943 the Kudzu Club of America could boast of 20,000 members, all devotees of this wonder plant.

But now the plant has been designated a weed by the Department of Agriculture because kudzu grows so fast (fifty feet a year, a foot a day during the growing season) and so deep (roots go down twenty feet) that it smothers everything else. Uncontrolled, it is a menace.

85. On Hospitality

Anonymous

A man attending a crowded church service refused to take off his hat when asked to do so by the ushers. Others also asked him to remove his hat, but he remained obstinate.

The preacher was perturbed, too, and waited for the man after the service. He told the man that the church was quite happy to have him as a guest, and invited him to join the church, but he explained the traditional decorum regarding men's hats and said, "I hope you will conform to that practice in the future."

"Thank you," said the man. "And thank you for taking time to talk to me. It is good of you to invite me to join the congregation. In fact, I joined it three years ago and have been coming regularly ever since, but today is the first time that anyone paid attention to me.

"After being an unknown for three years, today, by simply keeping on my hat, I have had the pleasure of talking with the ushers. And now I have a conversation with you, who have always appeared too busy to talk to me before."

What do you do to make strangers welcome? Are you too busy?

86. Too Stupid to Learn

Anonymous

One day a partially deaf boy came home from school with a note. It suggested that his parents take him out of school. The note said that the boy was "too stupid to learn."

When the boy's mother read the note, she said, "My son Tom isn't 'too stupid to learn.' I'll teach him myself."

When Tom died many years later, the people of our nation paid tribute to him by turning off the nation's lights, which Tom had invented, for one full minute.

Thomas Alva Edison invented not only the light bulb we read by, but also the motion picture we watch and the record player we listen to. He has more than 1,000 patents to his credit.

87. God Searches for Us

Anonymous

You may remember the story of Helen of Troy. According to legend, this beautiful queen was captured and carried away and became a victim of amnesia. She became a prostitute in the streets. She didn't know her name or the fact that she came from royal blood. But back in her homeland, friends didn't give up on her return. An old friend believed she was alive and went to look for her. He never lost faith.

One day while wandering through the streets, he came to a waterfront and saw a wretched woman in tattered clothes with deep lines across her face. There was something about her that seemed familiar, so he walked up to her and said, "What is your name?" She gave a name that was meaningless to him. "May I see your hands?" he pursued. She held her hands out in front of her, and the young man gasped, "You are Helen! You are Helen! Do you remember?"

She looked up at him in astonishment. "Helen!" he yelled out. Then the fog seemed to clear. There was recognition in her face. The light came on! She discovered her lost self, put her arms around her old friend and wept. She discarded the tattered clothes and once more became the queen she was born to be.

God searches for you in the same way. He uses every method possible to look for you and try to convince you of your worth to him.

88. The Trouble with Conformity

Earl Nightingale

I guess everyone has heard the remarkable stories about the lemmings—rugged little animals about the size of mice that, according to legends from Europe, occasionally migrate by the millions for days and nights until they reach the coast. When they reach the sea, they just keep on going, swimming straight out until they drown.

We hear a curious story like that, and we wonder why such a thing happens. There are several theories about it, one of which claims it's nature's way of regulating the lemming population—which isn't true, by the way.

Have you ever thought much about how people have a tendency to blindly follow another, or to conform so easily?

89. Devil's Clearance Sale

Anonymous

Reflect a moment on this legend that tells about the time the devil decided to close up shop in one part of the world and open up in another. A "going out of business" sale was announced. One of the first customers, being quite fascinated with the various evil instruments on display, noticed that of all the devil's tools, the highest priced one was called "discouragement."

"Why is that one so expensive?" he inquired.

"Quite simple," replied the devil. "It's my favorite. With the tool of discouragement I can pry into almost everyone's life and cause all kinds of damage."

90. In Community Is Strength

Anonymous

A pastor in a country parish heard that one of his parishioners was going about announcing that he would no longer attend church services. His rebellious parishioner was advancing the familiar argument that he could communicate just as easily with God out in the fields with the natural setting as his place of worship.

One winter evening the pastor called on this reluctant member of his flock for a friendly visit. The two men sat before the fireplace making small talk, but studiously avoiding the issue of church attendance. After some time, the pastor took the tongs from the rack next to the fireplace and pulled a single coal from the fire. He placed the glowing ember on the hearth.

The two men watched as the coal quickly ceased burning and turned an ashen gray, while the other coals in the fire continued to burn brightly. The pastor remained silent. "I'll be at services next Sunday," said the parishioner.

91. Loving Your Enemies

Anonymous

Abraham Lincoln tried to love, and left for all history a magnificent drama of reconciliation. When he was campaigning for the presidency, one of his arch-enemies was a man named Edwin McMasters Stanton. For some reason, Stanton hated Lincoln. He used every ounce of his energy to degrade him in the eyes of the public. So deep-rooted was Stanton's hate for Lincoln that he uttered unkind words about his physical appearance, and sought to embarrass him at every point with the bitterest diatribes. But in spite of this, Lincoln was elected the sixteenth president of the United States of America.

Then came the period when he had to select his cabinet, which would consist of the persons who would be his most intimate associates in implementing his programs. He started choosing men here and there for the various positions.

The day finally came for Lincoln to select the all-important post of secretary of war. Can you imagine whom Lincoln chose to fill this post? None other than the man named Stanton. There was an immediate uproar in the president's inner circle when the news began to spread. Advisor after advisor was heard saying, "Mr. President, you are making a mistake. Do you know this man Stanton? Are you familiar with all the ugly things he said about you? He is your enemy. He will seek to sabotage your programs. Have you thought this through, Mr. President?"

Mr. Lincoln's answer was terse and to the point: "Yes, I know Mr. Stanton. I am aware of all the terrible things he has said about me. But after looking over the nation, I find he is the best man for the job." So Stanton became Abraham Lincoln's secretary of war, and rendered an invaluable service to his nation and to his president.

Not many years later, Lincoln was assassinated. Many laudable things were said about him. But of all the great statements made about Abraham Lincoln, the words of Stanton remain among the greatest. Standing near the dead body of the man he once hated, Stanton referred to him as one of the greatest men that ever lived and said, "He now belongs to the ages."

If Lincoln had hated Stanton, both men would have gone to their graves as bitter enemies. But through the power of love Lincoln transformed an enemy into a friend. This is the power of redemptive love.

92. On Wealth

Anonymous

One day an Indian boy found a large pearl, which he thought to be priceless. Now he knew his worries were over. He would never have to work again in his life.

But when the boy tried to sell the pearl, the buyers put him off. In the days ahead the boy was attacked several times. Now he knew the pearl buyers were out to rob him and possibly kill him. He had a choice to make—between the pearl and his life.

With the pearl buyers looking on, the boy went down to the beach, took the pearl, and threw it into the sea as far as he could.

What hold do material possessions have on you?

93. The Rabbi's Gift

Anonymous

There was a famous monastery that had fallen on hard times. Formerly its many buildings were filled with young monks, and its big church resounded with the singing of the chant, but now it was nearly deserted. People no longer came there to be nourished by prayer. A handful of old monks shuffled through the cloisters and praised their God with heavy hearts.

On the edge of the monastery woods, an old rabbi had built a little hut. He would come there from time to time to fast and pray. No one ever spoke with him, but whenever he appeared, the word would be passed from monk to monk: "The rabbi walks in the woods." And, for as long as he was there, the monks would feel sustained by his prayerful presence.

One day the abbot decided to visit the rabbi and to open his heart to him. So after the morning Eucharist, he set out through the woods. As he approached the hut, the abbot saw the rabbi standing in the doorway, his arms outstretched in welcome. It was as though he had been waiting there for some time. The two embraced like long-lost brothers. Then they stepped back and just stood there, smiling at one another with smiles their faces could hardly contain.

After a while the rabbi motioned the abbot to enter. In the middle of the room was a wooden table with the scriptures open on it. They sat there for a moment, in the presence of the book. Then the rabbi began to cry. The abbot could not contain himself. He covered his face with his hands and began to cry, too. For the first time in his life, he cried his heart out. The two men sat there like lost children, filling the hut with their sobs and wetting the wood of the table with their tears.

After the tears had ceased to flow and all was quiet again, the rabbi lifted his head. "You and your brothers are serving God with heavy hearts," he said. "You have come to ask a teaching of me. I will give you this teaching, but you can only repeat it once. After that, no one must say it aloud again."

The rabbi looked straight at the abbot and said, "The messiah is among you." For a while, all was silent. Then the rabbi said, "Now you must go." The abbot left without a word and without ever looking back.

The next morning, the abbot called his monks together in the chapter room. He told them he had received a teaching from "the rabbi who walks in the woods" and that this teaching was never again to be spoken aloud. Then he looked at each of his brothers and said, "The rabbi said that one of us is the messiah!"

The monks were startled by this. "What could it mean?" they asked themselves. "Is Brother John the messiah? Or Father Matthew? Or Brother Thomas? Am I the messiah? What could this mean?"

They were all deeply puzzled by the rabbi's teaching. But no one ever mentioned it again.

As time went by, the monks began to treat one another with a very special reverence. There was a gentle, wholehearted, human quality about them now, which was hard to describe but easy to notice. They lived with one another as men who had finally found something. But they prayed the scriptures together as men who were always looking for something. Occasional visitors found themselves deeply moved by the life of these monks. Before long, people were coming from far and wide to be nourished by the prayer life of the monks, while young men were asking, once again, to become part of the community.

In those days, the rabbi no longer walked in the woods. His hut had fallen into ruins. But somehow or other, the old monks who had taken his teaching to heart still felt sustained by his prayerful presence.

94. The Stonecutter

Anonymous

There are days when I go and look at a stonecutter hammering away at his rock, perhaps a hundred times without as much as a crack showing in it. Yet at the one hundred-and-first blow it will split in two, and I know it was not the last blow that did it, but all that had gone before.

95. On Perseverance

Anonymous

The "ovenbird" is common to Argentina. It gets its unusual name from the fact that it builds its nest in an oven-like shape.

Several years ago, a pair of these birds built their mud-and-straw nest on top of the monuments that adorn a main plaza in Buenos Aires. A crew of workmen removed the nest. The next year the birds returned and rebuilt the nest. Again workmen removed the nest. Once again the birds returned and rebuilt the nest. This time citizens insisted that the workmen let the nest stay.

How persevering are we in our efforts?

96. Your Easter

Anonymous

A college student was on a plane flying from Pittsburgh to her home. As she stared out of the plane window down at the green countryside below, her heart was heavy and tears were in her eyes.

She was a student returning home for the Easter holidays. Her first year of college was nearly over, and it was a disaster. She was convinced that life no longer held any real meaning for her. Her only ray of happiness lay in the fact that she would soon see the ocean, which she loved dearly.

As the plane touched down on the runway, the girl wondered what kind of Easter vacation was possible after having had such a difficult time in college.

Her grandmother met her at the gate, and the two of them drove to her home in complete silence. As they pulled into the driveway, the girl's only thought was getting to the ocean.

It was well after midnight when she arrived at the beach. What happened next is best described in her own words. She says, "I just sat there in the moonlight watching the waves roll up on the beach. Slowly my disastrous first year passed before my eyes, day by day, week by week, month by month. Then suddenly, the whole experience fell into place. It was over and past. I could forget about it forever, but at the same time I didn't want to forget it.

"The next thing I knew, the sun was rising in the east. As it did, I sensed my feelings starting to peak, just as a wave starts to peak before it breaks. That morning I, too, arose!

"It was as though my mind, heart and body were drawing strength from the ocean. All my old goals, dreams and enthusiasm came rushing back stronger than ever. I rose with the sun, got into my car and headed for home."

After her Easter vacation that student returned to college, picked up the broken pieces of her year, and fitted them back together again. In the short span of an Easter vacation, she had died and risen again. For the first time in her life she understood the practical meaning of Easter.

97. The Greatest Person

Anonymous

In ancient times a king decided to find and honor the greatest person among his subjects. A man of wealth and property was singled out. Another was praised for her healing powers, another for his wisdom and knowledge of the law. Still another was lauded for his business acumen. Many other successful people were brought to the palace, and it became evident that the task of choosing the greatest would be difficult.

Finally, the last candidate stood before the king. It was a woman. Her hair was white. Her eyes shone with the light of knowledge, understanding and love.

"Who is this?" asked the king. "What has she done?"

"You have seen and heard all the others," said the king's aide. "This is their teacher!"

The people applauded, and the king came down from his throne to honor her.

98. A Patch of Ripe Berries

Anonymous

A Hasidic parable concerns a hungry boy traveling with his father through a dense forest. Suddenly, the boy spots a patch of ripe berries and begins picking them and eating them.

When the hour grows dangerously late, the boy can't bring himself to leave the patch. What could the father do? He loved the boy in spite of his childish behavior.

The father says, "I will start out; you may stay a few minutes longer. But to make sure we don't get separated, keep calling, 'Father! Father!' I will answer you. But as soon as my voice begins to fade, come running."

Hasidic masters used this parable to teach the need to keep united to God in prayer.

99. A Crab-in Today

Charles Schultz

A "PEANUTS" cartoon shows Charlie Brown warning Snoopy not to go near Lucy's house. "She's having a 'Crab-in' today," says Charlie.

Instead of heeding Charlie's warning, Snoopy goes straight to Lucy's house and knocks on the door. When the unhappy Lucy appears, Snoopy gives her a great big kiss. Then he trots off, saying to himself, "That's how you break up a 'Crab-in.'"

100. See the Opportunity

Earl Nightingale

I remember a man who once bought a small railroad that had been losing money for years. He got it at a real bargain, but those who sold it to him secretly laughed at what they called his poor judgment. He closed the railroad, sold the rails and equipment at a good price, and found himself with thousands of acres of real estate that had formerly been right-of-way.

The former owners had looked at it as a losing railroad; he looked at it as an opportunity to acquire valuable land.

101. Truth and Parable

Anonymous

A rabbi was once asked, "Why does a parable possess such great influence?"

He replied, "I will explain this by way of a parable:

"Truth was accustomed to walk about as naked as Truth was born. No one allowed Truth to enter a home and everyone who encountered Truth ran away in fright.

"Truth felt greatly embittered and could find no resting place. One day Truth beheld Parable attired in colorful, expensive garments. Parable inquired, 'Why are you so dejected, my friend?'

"Truth replied, 'I am in a bad situation. I am old, very old, and no one cares to have anything to do with me.'

"'Nay,' retorted Parable, 'it is not because of your age that you are disliked by people. Look, I am as old as you are, and the older I grow, the more I seem to be loved. Let me disclose to you the secret of my apparent popularity. People enjoy seeing everything dressed up and somewhat disguised. Let me lend to you some of my garments, and you will see that people will like you as well.'

"Truth followed this counsel and dressed in the garments of Parable. Ever since then, Truth and Parable walked hand in hand, and everyone loves them both."

102. The Precious Gift of Stories

Anonymous

Once upon a time, centuries ago, a rich caliph gave a banquet in honor of the birth of his son. All the nobility brought costly gifts, except a young sage who came empty-handed. He explained to the caliph, "Today the young prince will receive many precious gifts, jewels and rare coins. My gift is different. From the time he is old enough to listen until manhood, I will come to the palace and tell him stories of our Arabian heroes. When he becomes our ruler, he will have learned justice and honesty."

This young sage kept his word during the ensuing years. For when the young prince at last became caliph, he was renowned for his wisdom and honor. To this day, an inscription on a scroll reads, "It was because of the seed sown by the tales."

103. Build More Bridges

Anonymous

There were two brothers living on adjoining farms who developed a bitter conflict. It was their first serious rift in forty years of farming side-by-side, sharing machinery, and trading labor and goods as needed. They had never had a quarrel—that is until now.

It began with a small misunderstanding that grew into a major difference, and finally exploded into a bitter exchange of words, followed by separation and silence.

One morning there was a knock on the back door of the elder brother John's house. He opened it to find a man with a carpenter's toolbox standing on the stoop. "I'm looking for a few days' work," said the itinerant carpenter. "Perhaps you might have some small jobs?"

"Well, I believe I do," said the older brother. "Look across the creek at that farm. That's my neighbor, in fact it's my younger brother's place. Last week there was a meadow between our farms, that is, until he took a bulldozer and punched a hole in the river levee. Now there's this creek between us. Well, he may have done this to spite me," said the older brother, "but I'll go him one better. See that pile of lumber over thar by the barn? I want you to build me a fence—an eight-foot-tall fence—so I won't have to look at his place no more. Okay?"

"I think I understand the situation," replied the carpenter. "Show me to your tool shed, and I'll do you a job that will please you."

John was going to town for supplies, so he helped the carpenter get the materials ready and headed off for the day.

The carpenter toiled all day, measuring, sawing, pounding nails. Around sunset, the farmer returned home just as the carpenter was finishing the project.

The farmer stood aghast, his jaw drooped. There was no fence, but a bridge. A bridge now spanned the creek! It was a terrific piece of woodworking too—handrails and all. And, to John's amazement, across the bridge came his younger brother, arms outstretched.

"You are quite a craftsman and a brother," said the younger brother, "to have built this bridge after all I've said."

The two brothers met in the middle of the bridge and warmly embraced one another. As they turned they saw the carpenter packing up his tools. "No, wait!" both brothers shouted. "Stay on a bit longer. We have some other projects to discuss with you."

The carpenter replied, "Thanks, but I must be moving on. You see, I have many other bridges that need building."

104. All People Are Significant

Anonymous

A student relates about a time her professor gave a pop quiz. She was a conscientious student and breezed through the questions. That is, until she read the last one: "What is the name of the woman who cleans this floor of the building?"

She knew the woman referred to in the question. She'd seen her many times. She was tall, dark-haired, probably in her 50s. But the student had to hand in her paper leaving the last question blank.

When another student complained and asked if the last question would count toward the grade, the professor replied,

"Absolutely! In your careers you will meet many people. All of them are significant! They deserve your attention and care, even if all you can do is smile and say hello."

It was an example the students never forgot. And, oh, the cleaning woman's name was Dorothy. We may never remember all the names, but when do we ever have an excuse not to care?

105. Only One Referee— His Conscience

Anonymous

The *Chicago Tribune* reported about a big high school soccer game between Wheaton Christian and Waubonsie Valley. Waubonsie was the bigger school, and its team had the better record. But it wasn't until late in the game that Waubonsie Valley took a 3–2 lead.

As the clock ticked toward the end of the game, Waubonsie Valley took another shot on the Wheaton goal. The goalie stopped the ball, then threw it to his team's star player, Rob, a senior, who was the school's all-time top scorer.

Rob moved the ball past the defenders until the goal was within his range. He faked the goalkeeper and kicked the ball into the goal tying the game.

The Wheaton fans erupted in cheers. Rob's goal had saved his team from defeat.

But Rob noticed something—the clock on the scoreboard behind the goal had ticked down to zero before he kicked the ball. After consulting with the referee, who had not noticed that time had expired and who had already left the field, Rob told his coach that Waubonsie Valley should get the victory. They agreed and told the opposing coach that his team actually won the game.

When interviewed later, Rob said he considered the situation not as a tough decision, but as an opportunity. Rob told a reporter, "Every time you have an opportunity to do right, you should be thankful." He continued, "For a person to know what is right, and then not to do it, that would be a sin."

Rob explained, "To have won the game—I mean, really who cares? Doing the right thing is more important. It lets you have peace. Every time you are lucky enough to be given the opportunity to do right, you shouldn't pass it up."

106. Look for the Gold

Anonymous

At one time Andrew Carnegie was the wealthiest man in America. He came from his native Scotland when he was a small boy, did a variety of odd jobs, and eventually ended up as the largest steel manufacturer in the United States (U.S. Steel). At one time he had forty-three millionaires working for him. In those days a millionaire was a rare person; conservatively speaking, a million dollars in those days would be equivalent to at least twenty million dollars today.

One day, a reporter asked Carnegie how it was that he had hired forty-three millionaires. Carnegie responded that the men had not been millionaires when they started working for him, but had become millionaires only as a result.

The reporter's next question was, "Well, how did you develop these men to become so valuable to you that you paid them that much money?" Carnegie replied that people are developed the same way gold is mined. When gold is mined, several tons of dirt and stone must be moved first to get an ounce of gold, but one doesn't go into the mine looking for dirt—one goes in looking for gold.

That's exactly the way managers need to view people. Don't look for the flaws, warts and blemishes. Look for the gold, not the dirt; the good, not the bad. Look for the positive aspects of life. Like everything else, the more good qualities we look for in people, the more we are going to find.

107. Whistle and the Boat Stops

Anonymous

While campaigning for election in Illinois, Abraham Lincoln was challenged by an individual who made many vague, noisy complaints, but offered no constructive criticism.

Lincoln, skilled in handling such feckless hecklers, quietly remarked, "My good friend here reminds me of when I was but a lad and an old steamboat used to run down the river. It had a four-foot boiler and a seven-foot whistle. Why, every time it whistled, the boat stopped running."

108. Selfishness Shrivels the Oak Tree

Anonymous

A young oak tree was growing tall and strong. It rejoiced when it bore its first crop of acorns. Then one day, it heard the rustling of a nearby bramble bush. "These forest trees are our greatest enemies," railed the bramble. "Look at all the space they take up. Just look at all the nourishment they take from the earth!"

Some moss, growing at the foot of the parent-oak, said to the bramble, "Oh, but see what beautiful shade they give! How cool and pleasant it is here, and how glad the poor animals are to lie down during the heat of the day, out from the blazing heat of the sun. And see how the birds build their nests among the sturdy branches."

The selfish bramble replied, "All I know is they absorb a lot of nourishment, and they spread themselves out as if the world belonged to them. Cut them down, I say, and let us brambles take over."

"But you are forgetting all the acorns the trees provide," chirped another voice. "We squirrels love them and so do the pigs. The oaks give them gladly and for nothing."

"There, you see," said the bramble. "For nothing! Why should they be giving things for nothing? When it comes to us brambles, we give blackberries, but, in return, we snag all we can with our thorns. I don't believe in giving anything away for nothing."

The young oak listened attentively and soon began asking itself, "Yeah, why should I give away my acorns? Why should I shelter all these creatures? What do they ever do for me?"

Thereafter, whenever the squirrels and the pigs scampered and rooted for acorns, and whenever the weary cows and deer came to rest beneath the branches, the young oak shook its branches and said, "Go away. You can't share in my acorns or rest in my shade anymore."

Slowly, the young oak's sap turned to poison. The mighty oak began to wither from the inside out. The seasons came and went as usual, but the massive oak shrank into itself. The wind whispered and the trees murmured, "Give, give, or how shall you receive? Bless, or there is no room for blessing."

But the oak tree still muttered to itself, "Why should I?" It had rotted by now, to the heartwood, and you can see its shriveled shell whenever you go into that part of the forest.

109. Dare Mighty Things!

Theodore Roosevelt

President Theodore "Teddy" Roosevelt gave a speech at Chicago's Hamilton Club on April 10, 1899, that has become an enduring source of wisdom:

> In the battle of life, it is not the critic who counts; nor the one who points out how the strong person stumbled, or where the doer of a deed could have done better. The credit belongs to the person who is actually in the arena; whose face is marred by dust and sweat and blood, who strives valiantly; who errs and comes short again and again, because there is no effort without error and shortcoming; who does actually strive to do deeds; who knows the great enthusiasms, the great devotion, spends oneself in a worthy cause; who at the best knows in the end the triumph of high achievement; and who at worst, if he or she fails, at least fails while daring greatly.
>
> Far better it is to dare mighty things, to win glorious triumphs even though checkered by failure, than to rank with those timid spirits who neither enjoy nor suffer much because they live in the gray twilight that knows neither victory nor defeat.

110. Excellence

Michael Angier

Excellence is never an accident. It is achieved only as a result of an unrelenting and vigorous insistence on the highest standards of performance. It requires an unswerving expectancy of quality from everyone.

Excellence is contagious. It infects and affects everyone. It charts the direction of a program. It establishes the criteria for planning. It provides zest and vitality. Once achieved, excellence has a talent for permeating every aspect of life.

Excellence demands commitment and a tenacious dedication. Once it is accepted and expected, it must be nourished and continually reviewed and renewed. It is a never-ending process of learning and growing. It requires a spirit of motivation and boundless energy. It is always the result of a creatively conceived and precisely planned effort.

Excellence inspires; it electrifies. It potentializes every phase of life. It unleashes an impact that influences every program, every activity, every person. To instill it is difficult; to sustain it, even more so. It demands imagination and vigor. But most of all, it requires a constant state of self-discovery and discipline.

Excellence is one's life-line. It is the most compelling answer to apathy and inertia. It energizes a stimulating and pulsating force. Once it becomes the expected standard of performance, it develops a fiercely driving and motivating philosophy of operation. Excellence is a state of mind put into action. It is a road map to success. When a climate of excellence exists, all things come easier.

Excellence is important because it is everything.

111. Team Building

Anonymous

A world-class violinist was on campus for an artist-in-residence program. While at lunch he was discussing what he perceived to be a similarity between management and great music.

Said the violinist, "I have glorious music, a splendid instrument and an exquisite bow. All I need to do is bring them all together and get out of the way."

112. Recipe for a Happy New Year

Anonymous

Take twelve fine, full-grown months; see that these are thoroughly free from old memories of bitterness, rancor and hate; cleanse them completely from every clinging spite; pick off all specks of pettiness and littleness; in short, see that these months are freed from all the past. Have them fresh and clean as when they first came from the great storehouse of time. Cut these months into thirty or thirty-one equal parts. Do not attempt to make up the whole batch at one time (so many persons spoil the entire lot this way), but prepare one day at a time.

Into each day put equal parts of faith, patience, courage, work (some people omit this ingredient and so spoil the flavor of the rest), hope, fidelity, tolerance, kindness, rest (leaving this out is like leaving the oil out of the salad dressing—don't do it), prayer, meditation and one well-selected resolution. Put in about one teaspoonful of good spirits, a dash of fun, a pinch of folly, a sprinkling of play and a heaping cupful of good humor.

113. No Room for a Farmer

Anonymous

In the late 1700s the manager of a large hotel in Baltimore refused lodging to a man dressed like a farmer. He turned the farmer away because he thought this fellow's shabby appearance would discredit the reputation of his distinguished hotel. The farmer picked up his bag and left without saying a further word to anyone.

Later that evening, the innkeeper discovered that he had turned away none other than the vice-president of the United States, Thomas Jefferson! Immediately, the manager sent a note of apology to the famed patriot, asking him to come back and be his guest in the hotel.

Jefferson replied by instructing the messenger as follows, "Tell him I have already reserved a room. I value his good intentions highly, but if he has no room for a common American farmer, then he has no room for the vice-president of the United States of America."

114. Your Greatest Fear

Anonymous

Barbara Walters has interviewed many of the people who have changed the world in their lifetime. And she says, surprisingly, that Cher is one "who says things that make me think: 'I must remember that.'"

Walters elaborates, "I asked Cher what was her greatest fear?"

Cher answered, "Personally, that I won't live my life as well as I know it could be lived, that I'll be stupid and not have guts and integrity, that I'll make choices that are safe."

Walters says, "I often think of those words because I get afraid sometimes that I will do something because it is safe."

115. The Courage of Confidence

Mickey Mantle

Ted Williams had a lot of guts. When he hit .406 in 1941 he came into the last day of the season with 179 hits in 448 official at bats. That's an average of just under .400—or .39955, to be exact. In baseball, if your average is more than halfway between .399 and .400—you are given the higher figure. So, Williams was listed at .400, and that's the way it would have gone into the record books, too.

His manager suggested that Williams sit out the doubleheader scheduled for the last day of the season to make sure that his average stayed at .400. It was a rare feat to hit .400 for a season (it hadn't been done for eleven years before that), and Williams was told not to take the chance of having a bad day and dropping his average a few points.

But Williams stated, "If I'm going to be the batting champion, I'm going to win it like a champion." He played both games of the double-header, and got six hits in eight times at bat to lift his average six points on the last day of the season, to .406. That took the courage of confidence.

116. Honest Abe's Honesty

Anonymous

At the age of twenty-four, Abraham Lincoln served as the postmaster of New Salem, Illinois, for which he was paid an annual salary of $55.70. Even then, twenty-four years before he would enter the White House, the backwoods rail-splitter was showing the type of character that earned him the nickname of "Honest Abe."

The New Salem Post Office was closed in 1836, but it was several years before an agent arrived from Washington to settle accounts with ex-postmaster Lincoln, now a struggling lawyer and not doing very well. The agent informed Lincoln that according to his records $17 was due the government. Abe crossed the room, opened an old trunk and took out a yellowed cotton sack bound with string. Untying the bag, he shook out the contents, and there was exactly $17. "Honest Abe" had been holding it untouched, in safekeeping, for all these years.

"I never use any man's money but my own," said Abraham Lincoln.

117. There Is More Beyond

Anonymous

Before Christopher Columbus set sail from Spain into the vast unknown, it was believed that the world ended not far beyond Gibraltar. Indeed, this belief was expressed in the Spanish royal motto that read, *Ne Plus Ultra*, meaning "There is no more beyond here."

But when Columbus returned from the New World, he had actually discovered new horizons. This made the royal motto meaningless, until Queen Isabella simply eliminated the first word. Thus the royal motto became, *Plus Ultra*, meaning "There is plenty more beyond."

We may think there are no more "new frontiers" left today. But one of the legacies left to us by John F. Kennedy is that he awakened us to the fact that "new frontiers" need not be geographical. They may be social, political or spiritual, wherever there is hatred, poverty, prejudice, apathy, despair or hopelessness. Yes, there is plenty more beyond!

118. Hasten Slowly

Anonymous

Titus, the emperor of Rome, had the symbol of a dolphin wound around an anchor inscribed on coins during his reign. The anchor represented delay and unchanging conviction. The dolphin was regarded as the swiftest and most mercurial creature of the sea. Together they symbolized the failure that comes from rushing into something, and the failure that is the result of hesitation or undue caution.

Through the years, the dolphin and the anchor have been used as his family crest, with the explanatory motto *Festina Lente*, "Hasten Slowly." It expresses moderation between two opposing ideas. It means the medium between acting too quickly and waiting too long.

119. Learn from Successful Failures

William Franklin Summerout

To improve your self-image, learn from successful failures. Ty Cobb was thrown out more times trying to steal bases than any other player in baseball history. Babe Ruth struck out more times than anyone in baseball history. And Hank Aaron, who broke Ruth's home-run and strikeout records, struck out more often than 99 percent of the players who make it to the majors. Nobody—but nobody—considers them failures, and few people even remember their failures. Virtually everyone remembers their successes.

Enrico Caruso's voice failed to carry the high notes so many times his voice teacher advised him to quit. Caruso kept singing and was recognized as the greatest tenor of his day. Thomas Edison's teacher called him a dunce, and he did fail over 14,000 times in his efforts to perfect the incandescent light. Abraham Lincoln was well known for his lack of success, but nobody considers him a failure. Albert Einstein and Werner von Braun both flunked courses in math. Henry Ford was broke at age 40. Vince Lombardi became the most revered football coach since Knute Rockne, but at age 43 he was only a line coach at Fordham University.

120. Prayer to Illuminate Understanding

Anonymous

A convention was called in 1787 in the fledgling United States of America to revise the Articles of Confederation. For weeks delegates reviewed ancient history and analyzed governmental structures of Europe, searching for insights. But nothing suited the circumstances of this infant nation. Finally, one of the distinguished delegates, Benjamin Franklin, addressed the gathering. Referring to their meager progress, Franklin said, "In the situation of this assembly, groping as it were in the dark to find political truth and scarcely able to distinguish the same when it is presented to us, how has it happened that we have not hitherto once thought of humbly applying to the Father of Lights to illuminate our understandings?"

Those early leaders were not all Christians, yet many of them believed in a sovereign God and sought his wisdom in the affairs of state.

ACKNOWLEDGMENTS

This book is the fruition of years of reading, listening and transcribing stories from many and varied sources. I thank the authors and publishers who have given their generous cooperation and permission to include these stories in this collection. Further reproduction without permission is prohibited.

Every effort has been made to acknowledge the proper source for each story; regrettably, I am unable to give proper credit to every story. When the proper source becomes known, proper credit will be given in future editions of this book.

#1: **Cure for Sorrow,** Anonymous
     Source Unknown

#2: **Giving Calhoun the Ball,** Anonymous
     Source Unknown

#3: **Lost His Doxology,** Fred Craddock
     As One Without Authority,
     Abingdon Press, Nashville, Tenn., 1979.

#4: **The Acorn Planter,** Jean Giono
     The Man Who Planted Trees,
     Chelsa Green Publishing, Chelsa, Vt., 1985 (adapted).

#5: **Patience to Learn,** Anonymous
     Soundings, Vol. 3, #7,
     The Economics Press,
     12 Daniel Road, Fairfield, NJ 07006.
     Reprinted with permission.

#6: **Mystery of God,** William Jennings Bryan
     Source Unknown

#7: **Legend of the Thorn Bird,** Colleen McCullough
The Thorn Birds,
Avon Books, 1978.

#8: **St. Francis and the Novice,** Anonymous
Source Unknown

#9: **Love for Others: A Hasidic Story,** Anonymous
Source Unknown

#10: **Refusing to Accept Failure,** Anonymous
Source Unknown

#11: **Parable of the Cave,** Paula Ripple
Walking With Loneliness,
Ave Maria Press, Notre Dame, Ind., 1982.

#12: **On Judging Others,** Anonymous
Source Unknown

#13: **On Compassion,** Anonymous
Source Unknown

#14: **Pray Without Ceasing,** Anonymous
Source Unknown

#15: **Telling One's Own Story,** Anonymous
Source Unknown

#16: **The Watermelon Hunter,** Anonymous
Source Unknown

#17: **The Sorrow Tree,** Anonymous
Source Unknown

#18: **The Gnarled Old Oak Tree,** Brian Cavanaugh, T.O.R.
Human Development, Vol. 8, #4,
42 Kirkland Street, Cambridge, MA 02138.
Reprinted with permission.

#19: **The Three Student Devils,** Anonymous
Source Unknown

#20: **Answer to Prayer,** Anonymous
Source Unknown

#21: **Story to Heal,** Martin Buber
Source Unknown

#22: **The Samurai and the Tea Master,** Brian Cavanaugh, T.O.R
Human Development, Vol. 8, #2,
42 Kirkland Street, Cambridge, MA 02138.
Reprinted with permission.

#23: **Where Am I Going?,** Anonymous
Christopher News Notes, November 1983,
12 East 48th Street, New York, NY 10017.
Reprinted with permission.

#24: **New Angles—A Fresh Outlook?,** Anonymous
Christopher News Notes, April, 1978,
12 East 48th Street, New York, NY 10017.
Reprinted with permission.

#25: **God Made Part of Me,** Anonymous
Christopher News Notes, April, 1978,
12 East 48th Street, New York, NY 10017.
Reprinted with permission.

#26: **Make a Difference, #1,** Anonymous
Christopher News Notes, March, 1979,
12 East 48th Street, New York, NY 10017.
Reprinted with permission.

#27: **A Donkey, a Rooster and a Lamp,** Anonymous
Source Unknown

#28: **Make a Difference, #2,** Anonymous
Source Unknown

29: **The Magic Castle,** Vernon Howard
New Life Foundation, 1984.
Reprinted with permission.

#30: **Improve Gifts and Talents,** Anonymous
Source Unknown

#31: **On a Journey,** Anonymous
Source Unknown

#32: **Obstacles?...Deal with Them Now,** Anonymous
Source Unknown

#33: **The Face in the Window,** Anonymous
Source Unknown

#34: **My Crowd at Last,** Anonymous
Source Unknown

#35: **I Created You!,** Anonymous
Fr. Roland Faley, T.O.R.
Baccalaureate Homily,1985
St. Francis University, Loretto, PA 15940

#36: **Peak Experience,** Anonymous
Source Unknown

#37: **Grains of Caring,** Anonymous
Source Unknown

#38: **Heaven and Hell,** Anonymous
Source Unknown

#39: **The Farmer and the Pumpkin,** Earl Nightingale
INSIGHT #14. Excerpted with permission from *INSIGHT*®
the monthly audiocassette program by Earl
Nightingale. © 1984 by Nightingale-Conant Corp.,
7300 N. Lehigh Ave., Chicago, IL 60648.

#40: **Attention...,** Anonymous
Source Unknown

#41: **So Wise,** Anonymous
Source Unknown

#42: **Always Be Alert,** Anonymous
Source Unknown

#43: **Fact, Faith and Feeling,** Anonymous
Source Unknown

#44: **Three Questions,** Anonymous
Source Unknown

#45: **The Moso Bamboo,** Joel Weldon
Joel Weldon & Associates,
7975 N. Hayden Road, D-261,
Scottsdale, AZ 85258.
Reprinted with permission.

#46: **Attitude at Work,** Anonymous
Source Unknown

#47: **Light Too Bright,** Anonymous
Source Unknown

#48: **Eagle...or Prairie Chicken?,** Anonymous
Christopher News Notes, issue unknown,
12 East 48th Street,
New York, NY 10017.
Reprinted with permission.

#49: **Take Action,** Anonymous
Source Unknown

#50: **Heroes,** Anonymous
Source Unknown

#51: **Brother Jeremiah and Christian Service,** Anonymous
Soundings, issue unknown,
The Economics Press,
12 Daniel Road, Fairfield, NJ 07006.
Reprinted with permission.

#52: **Prayer Methods,** Anonymous
Source Unknown

#53: **Encouragement,** Anonymous
Source Unknown

#54: **Merchant of Death,** Anonymous
Source Unknown

#55: **Tell Them, Now,** Anonymous
Soundings, Vol. A, #1,
The Economics Press,
12 Daniel Road, Fairfield, NJ 07006.
Reprinted with permission.

#56: **The Lowly Paper Clip,** Anonymous
Source Unknown

#57: **Attitude Changes Everything,** Anonymous
Source Unknown

#58: **Find Someone in Need,** Anonymous
Source Unknown

#59: **Opportunity,** Anonymous
Source Unknown

#60: **Growing Older,** Anonymous
Soundings, May 1986,
The Economics Press,
12 Daniel Road, Fairfield, NJ 07006.
Reprinted with permission.

#61: **Where to Hide God?,** Anonymous
Source Unknown

#62: **Remember, You Must Die,** Anonymous
Source Unknown

#63: **Legend of the Trees,** Anonymous
Source Unknown

#64: **Handling Criticism,** Anonymous
Source Unknown

#65: **Diagnosing…Check the Size,** Anonymous
Source Unknown

#66: **Essence of Tact,** Anonymous
Source Unknown

#67: **No Talent,** Anonymous
Soundings, June 1986,
The Economics Press,
12 Daniel Road, Fairfield, NJ 07006.
Reprinted with permission.

#68: **How to Get to Heaven,** Anonymous
Source Unknown

#69: **Now That's Motivation,** Zig Ziglar
See You at the Top,
Pelican Publishing, Gretna, LA, 18984.

#70: **Balance,** Anonymous
Source Unknown

#71: **How We Look at Things,** Anonymous
Source Unknown

#72: **Learn from Mistakes,** Anonymous
Source Unknown

#73: **Notice and Observe Others,** Anonymous
Source Unknown

#74: **On Being a Saint,** Anonymous
Source Unknown

#75: **On Heaven,** Anonymous
Source Unknown

#76: **The Ten Commandments,** Anonymous
Source Unknown

#77: **Sadness in Beauty,** Anonymous
Source Unknown

#78: **Loneliness,** Anonymous
Source Unknown

#79: **Be a Flame,** Aesop
Aesop's Fables

#80: **Three Sons with Special Talents,** William J. Bausch
StoryTelling: Imagination and Faith,
Twenty-Third Publications,
185 Willow Street, Mystic, Conn.,
© 1984 by William J. Bausch.
Reprinted with permissions. All rights reserved.

#81: **Make Life an Adventure,** Roger Dawson
INSIGHT, October 1986, Excerpted with permission
from *INSIGHT*® the monthly audiocassette program by
Earl Nightingale. © 1986 by Nightingale-Conant
Corp., 7300 N. Lehigh Ave., Chicago, IL 60648.

#82: **Follower...or Disciple?,** Anonymous
Source Unknown

#83: **God Is Within You,** Anonymous
Source Unknown

#84: **Kudzu—Wonder or Menace?,** Anonymous
Three Minutes a Day, 1986, The Christophers,
12 East 48th Street, New York, NY 10017.
Reprinted with permission.

#85: **On Hospitality,** Anonymous
Three Minutes a Day, 1986, The Christophers,
12 East 48th Street, New York, NY 10017.
Reprinted with permission.

#86: **Too Stupid to Learn,** Anonymous
Source Unknown

#87: **God Searches for Us,** Anonymous
Source Unknown

#88: **The Trouble with Conformity,** Earl Nightingale
INSIGHT # 49. Excerpted with permission from
INSIGHT® the monthly audiocassette program by Earl
Nightingale. © 1986 by Nightingale-Conant Corp.,
7300 N. Lehigh Ave., Chicago, IL 60648.

#89: **Devil's Clearance Sale,** Anonymous
Source Unknown

#90: **In Community Is Strength,** Anonymous
Source Unknown

#91: **Loving Your Enemies,** Anonymous
Source Unknown

#92: **On Wealth,** Anonymous
Source Unknown

#93: **The Rabbi's Gift,** Anonymous
Source Unknown

#94: **The Stonecutter,** Anonymous
Source Unknown

#95: **On Perseverance,** Anonymous
Source Unknown

#96: **Your Easter,** Anonymous
Source Unknown

#97: **The Greatest Person,** Anonymous
Soundings, Vol. 3, #10,
The Economics Press,
12 Daniel Road, Fairfield, NJ 07006
Reprinted with permission.

#98: **A Patch of Ripe Berries,** Anonymous
Source Unknown

#99: **A Crab-in Today,** Charles Schultz
Source Unknown

#100: **See the Opportunity,** Earl Nightingale
INSIGHT, #59 (originally titled "The Right Time").
Excerpted with permission from *INSIGHT*® the monthly
audiocassette program by Earl Nightingale. ©1987 by
Nightingale-Conant Corp., 7300 N. Lehigh Ave.,
Chicago, IL 60648.

#101: **Truth and Parable,** Anonymous
Source Unknown

#102: **The Precious Gift of Stories,** Anonymous
Source Unknown

#103: **Build More Bridges,** Anonymous
Source Unknown

#104: **All People Are Significant,** Anonymous
Source Unknown

#105: **Only One Referee—His Conscience,** Anonymous
Source Unknown

#106: **Look for the Gold,** Anonymous
Source Unknown

#107: **Whistle and the Boat Stops,** Anonymous
Source Unknown

#108: **Selfishness Shrivels the Oak Tree,** Anonymous
Source Unknown

#109: **Dare Mighty Things!,** Theodore Roosevelt
Hamilton Club, Chicago, Ill., April 10, 1899

#110: **Excellence,** Michael Angier
Success Strategies™ (adapted), www.SuccessNet.org
Win-Win Way, PO Box 2048,
So. Burlington VT 05407.
Used with permission.

#111: **Team Building,** Anonymous
Source Unknown

#112: **Recipe for a Happy New Year,** Anonymous
Source Unknown

#113: **No Room for a Farmer,** Anonymous
Source Unknown

#114: **Your Greatest Fear,** Anonymous
Source Unknown

#115: **The Courage of Confidence,** Mickey Mantle
The Courage of Confidence
Bantam Books, New York, N.Y., 1964, p. 91.

#116: **Honest Abe's Honesty,** Anonymous
Source Unknown

#117: **There Is More Beyond,** Anonymous
Source Unknown

STORYTELLING READING LIST

Aesop's Fables. London: Bracken Books, 1986.

Allison, Christine, ed. *Teach Your Children Well.* New York: Bantam-Delacorte Press, 1993.

Arcodia, Charles. *Stories for Sharing.* Newtown, Australia: E.J. Dwyer, Ltd., 1991.

Armstrong, David. *Managing by Storying Around: A New Method of Leadership.* New York: Doubleday Currency Book, 1992.

Aurelio, John. *Story Sunday.* New York: Paulist Press, 1978.

———. *Fables for God's People.* New York: Crossroad, 1988.

———. *Colors! Stories of the Kingdom.* New York: Crossroad, 1993.

Ausubel, Nathan, ed. *A Treasury of Jewish Folklore.* New York: Crown Publishers, 1948.

Baldock, John. *The Little Book of Sufi Wisdom.* Rockport, Mass.: Element Books, 1995.

Bausch, William. *Storytelling: Imagination and Faith.* Mystic, Conn.: Twenty-Third Publications, 1984.

———. *A World of Stories for Preachers and Teachers.* Mystic, Conn.: Twenty-Third Publications, 1998.

Benjamin, Don-Paul and Ron Miner. *Come Sit with Me Again: Sermons for Children.* New York: The Pilgrim Press, 1987.

Bennett, William J., ed. *The Book of Virtues: A Treasury of Great Moral Stories.* New York: Simon and Schuster, 1993.

———. *The Moral Compass: Stories for a Life's Journey.* New York: Simon and Schuster, 1995.

Bettelheim, Bruno. *The Uses of Enchantment.* New York: Vintage Books, 1977.

Bleefeld, Rabbi Bradley R. and Robert L. Shook. *Saving the World Entire: And 100 Other Beloved Parables from the Talmud.* New York: Penguin Putnam/Plume, 1998.

Bodo, Murray, O.F.M. *Tales of St. Francis: Ancient Stories for Contemporary Living.* New York: Doubleday, 1988.

Bradt, Kevin M., S.J. *Story as a Way of Knowing*. Kansas City: Sheed and Ward, 1997.

Brody, Ed, Jay Goldspinner, et al., eds. *Spinning Tales, Weaving Hope: Stories, Storytelling and Activities for Peace, Justice and the Environment*. 2nd edition. New Society Publishers, PO Box 189, Gabriola Island, BC V0R 1X0 Canada, 1992, 2002.

Buber, Martin. *Tales of the Hasidim: Later Masters*. New York: Schocken Books, 1948.

———. *Tales of the Hasidim: Early Masters*. New York: Schocken Books, 1975.

Canfield, Jack and Mark V. Hansen. *Chicken Soup for the Soul*. Deerfield Beach, Fla.: Health Communications, Inc., 1993.

———. *A 2nd Helping of Chicken Soup for the Soul*. Deerfield Beach, Fla.: Health Communications, Inc., 1995.

———. *A 3rd Helping of Chicken Soup for the Soul*. Deerfield Beach, Fla.: Health Communications, Inc., 1996.

Canfield, Jack, Mark V. Hansen and Barry Spilchuk. *A Cup of Chicken Soup for the Soul*. Deerfield Beach, Fla.: Health Communications, Inc., 1996.

Canfield, Jack, Mark V. Hansen, Jennifer Read Hawthorne and Marci Shimoff. *Cup of Chicken Soup for the Woman's Soul*. Deerfield Beach, Fla.: Health Communications, Inc., 1996.

Canfield, Jack, Mark V. Hansen and Patty Hansen. *Condensed Chicken Soup for the Soul*. Deerfield Beach, Fla.: Health Communications, Inc., 1996.

Canfield, Jack, Mark V. Hansen, Hanoch McCarty and Meladee McCarty. *A 4th Course of Chicken Soup for the Soul*. Deerfield Beach, Fla.: Health Communications, Inc., 1997.

Canfield, Jack, Mark V. Hansen and Kimberly Kirkberger. *Chicken Soup for the Teenage Soul*. Deerfield Beach, Fla.: Health Communications, Inc., 1997.

Canfield, Jack, Mark V. Hansen, Patty Aubery and Nancy Mitchell. *Chicken Soup for the Christian Soul*. Deerfield Beach, Fla.: Health Communications, Inc., 1997.

Carroll, James. *Wonder and Worship*. New York: Newman Press, 1970.

Cassady, Marsh. *Storytelling: Step by Step*. San Jose, Calif.: Resource Publications, 1990.

————. *The Art of Storytelling: Creative Ideas for Preparation and Performance*. Colorado Springs: Meriwether Publishing Ltd., 1994.

Castagnola, Larry, S.J. *More Parables for Little People*. San Jose, Calif.: Resource Publications, 1987.

Cattan, Henry. *The Garden of Joys: An Anthology of Oriental Anecdotes, Fables and Proverbs*. London: Namara Publications, Ltd., 1979.

Cavanaugh, Brian, T.O.R. *The Sower's Seeds: One Hundred Inspiring Stories for Preaching, Teaching and Public Speaking*. Mahwah, N.J.: Paulist Press, 1990.

————. *More Sower's Seeds: Second Planting*. Mahwah, N.J.: Paulist Press, 1992.

————. *Fresh Packet of Sower's Seeds: Third Planting*. Mahwah, N.J.: Paulist Press, 1994.

————. *Sower's Seeds Aplenty: Fourth Planting*. Mahwah, N.J.: Paulist Press, 1996.

————. *Sower's Seeds of Virtue: Stories of Faith, Hope and Love*. Mahwah, N.J.: Paulist Press, 1997.

————. *Sower's Seeds of Encouragement: Stories of Hope, Humor and Healing*. Mahwah, N.J.: Paulist Press, 1998.

Chapman, H.S., ed. *1001 One Minute Stories*. Boston: Perry Mason Co., 1927.

Chappell, Stephen, O.S.B. *Dragons and Demons, Angels and Eagles: Morality Tales for Teens*. St. Louis: Liguori Publications, 1990.

Charlton, James and Barbara Gilson, eds. *A Christmas Treasury of Yuletide Stories and Poems*. New York: Galahad Books-LDAP, 1992.

Chinnen, Allan B. M.D. *Once Upon a Midlife*. New York: Jeremy P. Tarcher-Putnam Book, 1992.

————. *Beyond the Hero*. New York: Jeremy P. Tarcher-Putnam Book, 1993.

Colainni, James F., Sr., ed. *Sunday Sermons Treasury of Illustrations*. Pleasantville, N.J.: Voicings Publications, 1982.

Colainni, James F., Jr., ed. *Contemporary Sermon Illustrations.* Ventor, N.J.: Italicus, Inc., 1991.

Colum, Padraic, ed. *A Treasury of Irish Folklore.* 2nd edition. New York: Crown Publishers, Inc., 1967.

Complete Grimm's Fairy Tales, The. New York: Pantheon Books, 1972.

Cornils, Stanley, ed. *34 Two-Minute Talks for Youth and Adults.* Cincinnati, Ohio: Standard Publications, 1985.

de Mello, Anthony, S.J. *The Song of the Bird.* India: Gujarat Sahitya Prakash, 1982.

———. *One Minute Wisdom.* New York: Doubleday and Co., 1986.

———. *Taking Flight.* New York: Doubleday, 1988.

———. *The Heart of the Enlightened.* New York: Doubleday, 1989.

———. *One Minute Nonsense.* Chicago: Loyola University Press, 1992.

———. *More One Minute Nonsense.* Chicago: Loyola University Press, 1993.

de Voragine, Jacobus. *The Golden Legend: Reading on the Saints, Volume 1.* Princeton, N.J.: Princeton University Press, 1993.

———. *The Golden Legend: Reading on the Saints, Volume II.* Princeton, N.J.: Princeton University Press, 1993.

Dosick, Wayne. *Golden Rules: The Ten Ethical Values Parents Need to Teach Their Children.* San Francisco: HarperCollins, 1995.

Erdoes, Richard and Alfonso Ortiz, eds. *American Indian Myths and Legends.* New York: Pantheon Books-Random House, 1984.

Evans, Ivor, ed. *Brewer's Dictionary of Phrase and Fable.* 14th edition. New York: Harper and Row, 1989.

Fahy, Mary. *The Tree That Survived the Winter.* Mahwah, N.J.: Paulist Press, 1989.

Farra, Harry. *The Little Monk.* Mahwah, N.J.: Paulist Press, 1994.

Feehan, James A., *Story Power!: Compelling Illustrations for Preaching and Teaching.* Originally published as *Stories for*

Preachers. Dublin: Mercier Press, 1988. San Jose, Calif.: Resource Publications, 1994.

Forest, Heather. *Wisdom Tales from Around the World.* Little Rock, Ark.: August House, 1996.

Frankel, Ellen. *The Classic Tales: 4,000 years of Jewish Lore.* Northvale, N.J.: Jason Aronson, 1989.

Gallehugh, Sue, Ph.D. and Allen Gallehugh. *Bedtime Stories for Grown-ups: Fairy Tale Psychology.* Deerfield Beach, Fla.: Health Communications, Inc., 1995.

Giono, Jean. *The Man Who Planted Trees.* Chelsea, Vt.: Green Publishing Co., 1985.

Goodier, Steve. *Riches of the Heart.* Divide, Colo.: Life Support System Publishing, 1999.

———. *One Minute Can Change Your Life.* Divide, Colo.: Life Support System Publishing, 1999.

———. *Prescription for Peace.* Divide, Colo.: Life Support System Publishing, 2000.

———. *Joy Along the Way.* Divide, Colo.: Life Support System Publishing, 2000.

———. *Touching Moments.* Divide, Colo.: Life Support System Publishing, 2001.

Greer, Colin and Herbert Kohl, eds. *A Call to Character.* New York: HarperCollins, 1995.

Griffith, Joe. *Speaker's Library of Business Stories, Anecdotes & Humor.* New York: Prentice-Hall/Barnes & Noble, 1990.

Guroian, Vigen. *Tending the Heart of Virtue: How Classic Stories Awaken a Child's Moral Imagination.* New York: Oxford University Press, 1998.

Hasler, Richard A. *God's Game Plan: Sports Anecdotes for Preachers.* Lima, Ohio: C.S.S. Publishing Company, Inc., 1990.

Haugaard, Erik Christian, trans. *Hans Christian Anderson: The Complete Fairy Tales and Stories.* New York: Anchor-Doubleday, 1974.

Hays, Edward. *Twelve and One-Half Keys.* Leavenworth, Kans.: Forest of Peace Books, 1981.

————. *Sundancer: A Mystical Fantasy.* Leavenworth, Kans.: Forest of Peace Books, 1982.

————. *The Ethiopian Tattoo Shop.* Leavenworth, Kans.: Forest of Peace Books, 1983.

————. *A Pilgrim's Almanac: Reflections for Each Day of the Year.* Leavenworth, Kans.: Forest of Peace Books, 1989.

————. *The Magic Lantern.* Leavenworth, Kans.: Forest of Peace Books, 1991.

————. *The Christmas Eve Storyteller.* Leavenworth, Kans.: Forest of Peace Books, 1992.

————. *Holy Fools and Mad Hatters.* Leavenworth, Kans.: Forest of Peace Books, 1993.

————. *The Quest for the Flaming Pearl.* Leavenworth, Kans.: Forest of Peace Books, 1994.

————. *The Old Hermit's Almanac: Daily Meditations for the Journey of Life.* Leavenworth, Kans.: Forest of Peace Books, 1997.

Henderschedt, James L. *The Magic Stone.* San Jose, Calif.: Resource Publications, Inc. (160 E. Virginia Street, S-290), 1988.

————. *The Topsy-Turvy Kingdom.* San Jose, Calif.: Resource Publications, Inc. (160 E. Virginia Street, S-290), 1990.

————. *The Light in the Lantern.* San Jose, Calif.: Resource Publications, Inc. (160 E. Virginia Street, S- 290), 1991.

————. *The Beggar's Bowl: Parables and Short Stories for Spiritual Preaching.* Bethlehem, Pa.: Faith Journey Creations (PO Box 4219), 1994.

————. *The Hammer Man.* Bethlehem, Pa.: Faith Journey Creations (PO Box 4219), 1995.

Holdcraft, Paul E., ed. *Snappy Stories for Sermons and Speeches.* Nashville: Abingdon Press, 1987.

Holt, David and Bill Mooney. *Ready-to-Tell Tales.* Little Rock, Ark.: August House, 1994.

Hughes, R. Kent. *1001 Great Stories & Quotes.* Wheaton, Ill.: Tyndale House, 1998.

Hunt, Angela Elwell. *The Tale of Three Trees: A Traditional Folktale.* Batavia, Ill.: Lion Publishing Corp., 1989 (1705 Hubbard Ave., Batavia, IL 60510).

Jaffe, Nina and Steve Zeitlin, eds. *While Standing on One Foot: Puzzle Stories and Wisdom Tales from the Jewish Tradition.* New York: Henry Holt, 1993.

Johnson, Miriam. *Inside Twenty-Five Classic Children's Stories.* New York: Paulist Press, 1986.

Juknialis, Joseph. *Winter Dreams and Other Such Friendly Dragons.* San Jose, Calif.: Resource Publications, Inc, 1979.

Kronberg, Ruthilde and Patricia C. McKissack. *A Piece of the Wind and Other Stories to Tell.* New York: Harper and Row, 1990.

————. *Clever Folk: Tales of Wisdom, Wit and Wonder.* Englewood, Colo.: Libraries Unlimited, Inc., 1993.

Kurtz, Ernest and Katherine Ketchman. *The Spirituality of Imperfection: Storytelling and the Journey to Wholeness.* New York: Bantam, 1992.

L'Estrange, Sir Rodger. *Fables of Aesop.* Drawings by Alexander Calder. New York: Dover Publications, 1967.

Levin, Meyer. *Classic Hasidic Tales.* New York: Dorset Press, 1985.

Levine, David, ed. *The Fables of Aesop.* New York: Dorset Press, 1989.

Lewis, Naomi, ed. *Cry Wolf and Other Aesop Fables.* New York: Oxford University Press, 1988.

Lieberman, Leo and Arthur Beringause. *Classics of Jewish Literature.* Secaucus, N.J.: Book Sales, Inc., 1988.

Lipman, Doug. *Improving Your Storytelling.* Little Rock, Ark.: August House Publishers, 1999.

Litherland, Janet. *Storytelling from the Bible.* Colorado Springs, Colo.: Meriwhether Publishing Ltd., 1991.

Livo, Norma J. and Sandra A. Rietz. *Storytelling: Process and Practice.* Littleton, Colo.: Libraries Unlimited, Inc., 1986.

————. *Storytelling Folklore Sourcebook.* Littleton, Colo.: Libraries Unlimited, Inc., 1991.

Lobel, Arnold. *Fables.* New York: HarperCollins, 1980.

Loder, Ted. *Tracks in the Snow: Tales Spun from the Manger.* San Diego, Calif.: LuraMedia, 1985.

Lufburrow, Bill. *Illustrations Without Sermons*. Nashville: Abingdon Press, 1985.

MacDonald, Margaret Read. *Peace Tales: World Folktales to Talk About*. Hamden, Conn.: Linnet Books, 1992.

Marbach, Ethel. *The White Rabbit: A Franciscan Christmas Story*. Cincinnati, Ohio: St. Anthony Messenger Press, 1984.

McArdle, Jack. *150 Stories for Preachers and Teachers*. Mystic, Conn.: Twenty-Third Publications, 1990.

McCarthy, Flor, S.D.B. *And the Master Answered....*Notre Dame, Ind.: Ave Maria Press, 1985.

McKenna, Megan and Tony Cowan. *Keepers of the Story*. Maryknoll, New York: Orbis Books, 1997.

Mellon, Nancy. *Storytelling and the Art of Imagination*. Rockport, New York: Element, Inc., 1992.

Meyer, Gabriel. *In the Shade of the Terebinth: Tales of a Night Journey*. Leavenworth, Kans.: Forest of Peace Publishing, 1994.

Miller, Donald. *The Gospel and Mother Goose*. Elgin, Ill.: Brethren Press, 1987.

National Storytelling Association, The. *Tales as Tools: The Power of Story in the Classroom*. Jonesborough, Tenn.: The National Storytelling Press, 1994.

————. *Many Voices: True Tales from America's Past*. Jonesborough, Tenn.: The National Storytelling Press, 1995.

————. *Storytelling* magazine. NSA, PO Box 309, Jonesborough, Tenn. 37659.

Nelson, Pat. *Magic Minutes*. Englewood, Colo.: Libraries Unlimited, Inc., 1993.

Newcombe, Jack. *A Christmas Treasury*. New York: Viking Press, 1982.

Newman, Louis I. *The Hasidic Anthology: Tales and Teachings of the Hasidim*. New York: Schocken Books, 1963 (4th printing, 1975).

Night the Stars Sang, The: The Wonder that Is Christmas. Tarrytown, New York: Gleneida Publishing Group-Triumph Books, 1991 (by special arrangement with Guidepost Books).

Nomura, Yushi. *Desert Wisdom: Sayings from the Desert Fathers.* New York: Image Books, 1984.

Norfolk, Bobby and Sherry. *The Moral of the Story: Folktales for Character Development.* Little Rock, Ark.: August House Publishers, 1999.

Paulus, Trina. *Hope For The Flowers.* Mahwah, N.J.: Paulist Press, 1972.

Pellowski, Anne. *The World of Storytelling.* Revised edition. New York: H. W. Wilson, 1990.

Polsky, Howard W. and Yaella Wozner. *Everyday Miracles: The Healing Wisdom of Hasidic Stories.* Northvale, N.J.: Jason Aronson Inc., 1989.

Powers, C.P., Isaias. *Nameless Faces in the Life of Jesus.* Mystic, Conn.: Twenty-Third Publications, 1981.

——. *Father Ike's Stories for Children.* Mystic, Conn.: Twenty-Third Publications, 1988.

Prather, Hugh and Gayle Prather. *Parables from Other Planets.* New York: Bantam Books, 1991.

Schwartz, Howard and Barbara Rush, eds. *The Diamond Tree: Jewish Tales from Around the World.* New York: HarperCollins, 1991.

Seuss, Dr. *Oh, the Places You'll Go!* New York: Random House, 1990.

Shah, Idries. *The Hundred Tales of Wisdom.* London: Octagon Press, 1978.

——. *Seeker After Truth.* London: Octagon Press, 1982, 1992.

——. *The Subtleties of the Inimitable Mulla Nasrudin* and *The Exploits of the Incomparable Mulla Nasrudin: Two Volumes in One.* London: Octagon Press, 1983.

——. *World Tales.* London: Octagon Press, 1991.

——. *Tales of the Dervishes: Teaching Stories of the Sufi Masters over the Past Thousand Years.* 1967. New York: Penguin–Arkana, first U.S. edition 1993.

Shea, John. *The Spirit Master.* Chicago: Thomas More Press, 1987.

Shedlock, Marie L. *The Art of the Story Teller.* 3rd edition. New York: Dover Publications, 1951.

Simpkinson, Charles and Anne Simpkinson, eds. *Sacred Stories: A Celebration of the Power of Stories to Transform and Heal.* San Francisco: HarperSanFrancisco, 1993.

Singer, Isaac Bashevis. *Stories for Children.* New York: Farrar, Straus, Giroux, 1984.

————. *The Image and Other Stories.* London: Jonathan Cape, Ltd., 1985.

Stanton, Sue. *Boston and the Feast of St. Francis.* Mahwah, N.J.: Paulist Press, 1994.

Stoddard, Sandol. *The Rules and Mysteries of Brother Solomon.* Mahwah, N.J.: Paulist Press, 1987.

Stone, Richard. *The Healing Art of Storytelling.* New York: Hyperion, 1996.

Sutherland, Zena and Myra Cohn Liningston, eds. *The Scott, Foresman Anthology of Children's Literature. Glenview,* Ill.: Scott, Foresman and Co., 1984.

Swindoll, Charles R. *The Tale of the Tardy Oxcart and 1501 Other Stories.* Nashville: Word Publishing, 1998.

Tazewell, Charles. *The Littlest Angel.* Nashville: Ideals Publishing, 1946.

Theophane the Monk. *Tales of a Magic Monastery.* New York: Crossroad, 1981.

Thoma, Clemens and Michael Wyschogrod, eds. *Parable and Story in Judaism and Christianity.* Mahwah, N.J.: Paulist Press, 1989.

Thompson, Stith. *The Folktale.* Los Angeles: The University of California Press, 1977.

Valles, Carlos G., S.J. *Tales of the City of God.* Chicago: Loyola University Press, 1993.

Van Dyke, Henry, James S. Bell, eds. *A Treasury of Christmas Stories.* Wheaton, Ill.: Harold Shaw Publishers, 1993.

Walker, Scott. *Glimpses of God: Stories that Point the Way.* Minneapolis, Minn.: Augsburg Fortress, 1997.

Ward, Benedicta, trans. *The Sayings of the Desert Fathers.* Kalamazoo, Mich.: Cistercian Publications, 1975 (revised 1984).

Weinreich, Beatrice Silverman, ed. *Yiddish Folktales.* Translated by Leonard Wolf. New York: Pantheon-Random House, 1988.

Wharton, Paul, ed. *Stories and Parables for Preachers and Teachers.* New York: Paulist Press, 1986.

White, William R., ed. *Speaking in Stories.* Minneapolis: Augsburg, 1982.

———. *Stories for Telling.* Minneapolis: Augsburg, 1986.

———. *Stories for the Journey.* Minneapolis: Augsburg, 1988.

———. *Stories for the Gathering.* Minneapolis: Augsburg, 1997.

Wiesel, Elie. *Souls on Fire: Portraits and Legends of Hasidic Masters.* New York: Summit Books, 1972.

———. *Somewhere a Master: Further Hasidic Portraits and Legends.* New York: Summit Books, 1981.

Wilde, Oscar. *The Happy Prince and Other Fairy Tales.* New York: Dover, 1992.

———. *The Fairy Tales of Oscar Wilde.* New York: Henry Holt and Co., 1993.

Yolen, Jane, ed. *Favorite Folktales from Around the World.* New York: Pantheon Books-Random House, 1986.

Zipes, Jack, ed. *Spells of Enchantment: The Wondrous Fairy Tales of Western Culture.* New York: Viking-Penguin, 1991.

———. *Aesop's Fables...and 200 Other Famous Fables.* New York: Signet Classic-Penguin, 1992.

Theme Index

The numbers after the theme refer to the story number, not the page number.

Also by Father Brian Cavanaugh, T.O.R.
Published by Paulist Press

MORE SOWER'S SEEDS: SECOND PLANTING
FRESH PACKET OF SOWER'S SEEDS: THIRD PLANTING
SOWER'S SEEDS APLENTY: FOURTH PLANTING
SOWER'S SEEDS OF VIRTUE (SPIRITUAL SAMPLER)
SOWER'S SEEDS OF ENCOURAGEMENT
SOWER'S SEEDS THAT NOURISH FAMILY VALUES

And for Children

MIRACLE OF THE POINSETTIA
with illustrations by Dennis Rockhill